An
AMERICAN
CRICKET
Odyssey

BETH SIMPSON AND MARK GREENSLADE

An AMERICAN CRICKET Odyssey

A JOURNEY INTO THE SOUL OF CRICKET IN THE UNITED STATES

pitch

First published by Pitch Publishing, 2025

1

pitch

Pitch Publishing
9 Donnington Park,
85 Birdham Road,
Chichester, West Sussex,
PO20 7AJ
www.pitchpublishing.co.uk
info@pitchpublishing.co.uk

A CIP catalogue record is available for this book
from the British Library.

ISBN 978 1 83680 167 2

Typesetting and origination by Pitch Publishing

FSC
www.fsc.org
MIX
Paper | Supporting
responsible forestry
FSC™ C016779

Printed and bound on FSC® certified paper in line with
our continuing commitment to ethical business practices,
sustainability and the environment.

Printed and bound in India by Replika Press Pvt. Ltd.

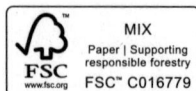

Contents

Introduction. 7

Departure Point. 11

1. The Gentlemen of Philadelphia 15

2. At Home with the Homies. 35

3. The New York Underground 59

4. The Cricket Junkies 83

5. The Long and Winding Road 118

6. Dreamers and Schemers 144

7. 'Just Play More'. 174

8. If you build it, will they come? 196

9. Into the Heartlands. 232

10. A Field in an Infertile Land 259

11. The Journey Home 276

Introduction

An American Cricket Odyssey – Why?

IT ALL began in the dying days of 2003. One of us had just lost their mother, the other – after decades – had just found their birth father. Both traversing, albeit in opposite directions, through a landscape of life change. After a number of evenings of mutual soul searching, an idea was floated: a road trip, next year sometime? Yes.

Except just a road trip seemed decadent, foolish and without purpose. There had to be an idea behind it.

We alighted on cricket. We had met and played against the Compton Homies and Popz. We knew something of the history of the game in the States and were curious what else there was to discover, what other stories we could find. We had a hunch there could be quite a lot.

Our hunch proved correct. Inevitably, one road trip in autumn 2004, as the country geared up for the first of what would be many 'Armageddon' elections, wasn't enough. In fact it barely scratched the surface. We had to come back, again. And again.

And so the odyssey stretched out over time. Real life interrupted our progress. The need to earn a living. New families. New relationships. We returned whenever time would allow. Things changed slowly in US cricket. The same old characters, faces. A cycle endlessly repeating itself.

Strangely the country's politics often seemed to move in step with the progress of its cricket. For every brave step forward, for every new dawn, there was a stumble and a fall back. We write this in February 2025 when the USA under its present regime seems determined to become a pariah state. If its cricketing governing body is suspended yet again by the ICC this year, it'll be for the fourth time since we started following this story. Corruption, greed, the hoarding of power and a failure of vision – governance in both US politics and cricket currently seems blighted by it.

That sounds quite depressing, doesn't it? But there have been brighter moments. What's spurred us on during what at times has seemed a thankless, doomed mission, have been the stories of the ordinary Americans who have fallen in love with the game, many from non-cricketing backgrounds. Their love of the sport and the simple pleasure that they take from it is truly inspiring and reminds us why we fell in love with it too. If that nebulous concept of the 'spirit of cricket' resides anywhere in the US game, it resides in them.

An American Cricket Odyssey isn't a definitive portrait. How could it be? The country, or more accurately continent, is just too large and varied to reduce to an easy snapshot. We didn't get to all the places we wanted to get to, nor include all the players and figures we wanted to meet. Emails and phone calls often went unanswered, trails often went cold. But we tried our best.

What we have tried to produce is a moving image over time of a country, a subculture/s that hopefully throws new light over the people making their way, carving a space for themselves and their sport in this country. We hope our outsiders' perspective has helped in this. We have tried to be balanced, and there will doubtless be those who will be infuriated by what we have written. To them we apologise in advance.

America is an inspiring, beautiful, astounding, profoundly moving country/idea that appeals to our higher purpose as human beings. But it's also deeply flawed, utterly exasperating, often incomprehensible to outsiders and at times spiteful and cruel. As is cricket. And yet we love both. But it's the potential of reaching that higher ground – mentally and spiritually – that drives us on in sport, in our lives as humans, even while we remain rooted to the spot.

The future of both US society and cricket depends on the willingness of its ordinary people to refuse to give in to the darkness, but to keep leaning up towards that light.

We hope you enjoy the journey.

Will Simpson and Mark Greenslade,

February 2025

Departure Point

A GREY, overcast day at the end of another damp English summer and we are about to witness a piece of sporting history – the debut first-class international tournament for the United States national cricket team. This is the first time the US are competing on an equal footing with the best Test-playing nations. And this is the very best. Australia. World champions. Undisputedly the greatest international side in the world.

The tournament in question is the ICC Champions Trophy, hardly a Mickey Mouse affair but still a sideshow to the 50-over World Cup. Started up in 1998 as a biennial event, one of the main ideas of the competition is to encourage cricket in the sport's so-called 'developing' nations – in theory it gives the likes of the US, Zimbabwe and Bangladesh practice against the big boys, sharpen their game and their appetite for big-time cricket. Already team

Bangladesh have graduated to full Test level. Having made it this far perhaps the US can follow in their footsteps?

It's a curious scene. The Rose Bowl is a new out of town sports stadium carved into the rolling Hampshire countryside with a ludicrously grandiose name (no one in Britain calls sports stadia 'bowls'), blustery autumnal English weather and an American team that are complete underdogs. The Aussies win the toss and put Team USA in to bat. Within an over they are already 3/2.

Despite some nice strokes by Steve Massiah, the US are soon in deep trouble. It's 16/4 as Rohan Alexander goes for 8. Tony Reid, a 42-year-old comes in and makes just 2. By 46/6 it's already looking like we're witnessing the lowest total in a Champions Trophy match unless the Aussies show some mercy. They don't. The US are all out for 65 with Jason Gillespie and Michael Kasprowicz grabbing four wickets each.

After lunch it takes the Australians all of 33 minutes and eight overs to surpass this meagre total. It's a massacre. In the post-match press conference Australian captain Ricky Ponting makes noises to the effect that he thinks the match has been a waste of time for all concerned. America's return, after the best part of a century, to the top table of international cricket has ended in utter humiliation.

It was a strange, unreal sort of day. It wasn't just the fact the game was done and dusted by 2pm, the crowd too was an odd mixture. Apart from the hardcore Australia fans, there was a smattering of interested locals and neutrals. But there were also more than a few US supporters, some even waving flags and chanting 'U-S-A'. Most of these were expats, many seemed to live in and around Southampton and almost all were supporting their national team with tongues firmly in cheeks. They knew the US team had little chance of producing an upset against the mighty Australians but were cheering them on regardless. The mere fact that the US had a cricket team, and that cricket was played in their homeland at all, seemed to tickle them enormously.

During this book's research period it's a standpoint that we've encountered time and again. To the uninitiated the idea that Americans, loud, brash, gum-chewing, baseball-loving Americans, play this genteel esoteric pastime is an absolute hoot. Both in the US and in Europe the most common reaction when we explain about the project has been an expression of surprise and a response along the lines of 'I didn't know they played it at all.' In the UK even most cricket fans are unaware of the game's long history in the US and its status as a mass spectator sport in the 19th century. In the States itself the game is so far under the radar that it's positively subterranean. The US sports media completely ignores it. Mention the word 'cricket' to the average American sports fan and many will simply assume you're making some reference to the insect species.

So it was with the idea of shedding some light upon US cricket's fascinating backstory and discovering for ourselves what its revival looked, sounded and smelt like that, three weeks after the debacle at the Rose Bowl, we embarked on the first stage of our odyssey into the heart of this subculture (or to be more accurate 'subcultures') that the world knows so little of. At this early stage our contacts were outnumbered by the many questions we had: How was the game kept alive in the US during the middle years of the 20th century? Why, given that it is operating in the richest economy in the world, is US cricket so impoverished? Why are some members of the national team so old? Is it true that George Washington played the game? Or that cricket was once played on the White House lawn?

And where to begin? We flew into Washington, but prior to our departure we had already gleaned that the city further up the East Coast had been a major centre for cricket in the 19th century. We'd also heard that there was a museum nearby that was entirely devoted to the sport, so one bright October morning we headed north to Philadelphia with a map, a packed lunch and a hunch that this might be a suitable starting point for our adventure.

1

The Gentlemen of Philadelphia

IF AMERICAN cricket has a spiritual home it lies in Philadelphia and in particular amid the neatly cut hedges and trim lawns of the city's north-western fringes, the locales of Germantown, Chestnut Hill and Main Line. For it is here that the game lasted longer than anywhere else in the US, where it survived as a regional subculture right up until World War One. Even today reminders of its one-time glory can be glimpsed in the grand clubhouses and elegantly maintained grounds that belong to Merion, Germantown and Philadelphia cricket clubs.

Most of the modern-day custodians of the game are able to furnish you with US cricket's one indisputable claim to fame – that the first international match, not just in cricket but in any sport, took place in 1844 between the United States and Canada. They might also tell you that the sport has a long and proud history in the US, that games drew crowds in their thousands in the 19th century and that England toured here in the 1850s. Cricket was a sport that was played in America throughout the 19th century, but its great failing lay in the fact that it never truly became an American sport.

The reasons for this are numerous. Undoubtedly the rise of baseball around the Civil War period was a major factor. Baseball was quicker to play – one game lasted just an hour or so compared to three to five days and, unlike cricket, required hardly any equipment. No need to erect stumps or roll out a wicket; baseball required just a bat, ball and something that could be utilised as a base. It was an ideal pastime for the thousands of soldiers that were stationed around the country during the Civil War, bored men with energy to spare in the long and tedious downtime between battles.

Cricket also carried with it a heavy whiff of the old country – i.e. England. Immigration to the States increased throughout the 19th century, reaching a peak in the first decade of the 20th. Increasingly migrants were arriving from southern and eastern Europe rather than Great Britain and thus had no interest in (or even knowledge of) this arcane English sport. In the decades after the civil war cricket increasingly found itself boxed in as an elite pastime played by English first- or second-generation immigrants.

Whilst there are still reports of games being played in Merion, Colorado and even Montana around 1900, by the end of the century the game had pretty much died out in the Midwest and much of the so-called American 'heartland'.

In Philadelphia though it was a different matter. For one thing the sport was played to a far higher standard in the city and its surrounding areas. A number of Philadelphian select teams toured England, playing against first-class counties in the years 1897, 1903 and 1908. The last tour in 1908 even saw the Philadelphians beat MCC. There were also regular tours by the so-called Gentlemen of Philadelphia, a combined team who toured England in 1884 and 1889.

The Philadelphia scene also boasted the most famous American cricketer of all time, John Barton King (commonly known as John Bart King), an all-rounder who developed a fearsome technique of swinging the ball, which he termed the angler. The star of the Philadelphians, three English tours, when King retired in 1916 US cricket lost its greatest ever ambassador and certainly the only player who could stand comparison with the great English and Australian Test players of the day.

The game in the town was also played and supported by a very specific social set. The largest and wealthiest clubs, all situated in the west of the city – Merion, Germantown, Philadelphia, Belmont – all drew their personnel and support from a leisured upper-middle class that self-consciously mimicked their English counterparts' genteel behaviour. For them, playing cricket was a social signifier, a way, in the words of the *Philadelphia Evening Bulletin* of 19 August 1872, that 'a gentleman can show his moral character' and 'learn lessons of self-control, patience, endurance and perseverance which he can obtain in no other way'.

Yet whilst it's correct that a haughty Anglophilia permeated much of Philadelphian cricket circles in the late 19th and early 20th centuries, certain clubs and individuals went out of their way to create a uniquely American cricketing identity. Foreigners were expressly forbidden from playing for the city's representative sides and the Young America club of Philadelphia was just one that banned non-Americans from playing for its teams. In the long run though, this stance proved to be unsustainable – Young America merged with nearby Germantown CC in 1890. Without a fresh influx of young players, year by year the demographics of Philadelphian cricketers grew older, clubs closed, and the scene gradually withered and died after World War One.

* * *

For anyone genuinely interested in the history of the game in America, the starting point lies miles to the west of Philadelphia at Haverford College. It is here one golden October morning in 2004, one of those triumphant truly autumnal days that seem perfectly balanced between summer and winter, that we find ourselves driving up the long leafy approach to the college campus. As if by magic, as we approach the entrance a number of white-clad figures are emerging from a pavilion to our left. It looks as if a game is going to be played.

We're here to visit the CC Morris Cricket Library, the foremost repository of artefacts and memorabilia about the game in the United States. We ask one of the men in white, a tubby guy in his 40s with a slight Scouse accent, where the museum is. It seems we've stumbled across the annual Toronto v British Officers game.

The British Officers aren't actually officers. Not anymore. The club was founded after World War One by a group of Brits who wanted to play the game with their US counterparts. These days they comprise a mixed bunch of expats from around the Test-playing nations. As the game is just beginning it seems like a good idea to find the library before we get too engrossed in proceedings.

So we tiptoe through the quadrangle, past scurrying squirrels and students clutching files, until we come to a church-like building. This must be it. The door is closed. We knock three times, and the door is opened by a small greyish man. 'Are you the curator?' we ask.

He is. Stuart McDougall is his name and he's only been at Haverford for the last eight months. The actual museum dates back to 1964 and is named after one of the last great cricketers that the college produced before the game died here after World War One.

The room inside is a treasure trove of books, videos, old blazers, ties and cards. There are the photos dating back to the 1860s and a horde of old *Wisdens* on the bookshelves. Mr McDougall is a gracious host chatting with us about the game and the history of cricket here at Haverford. He doesn't get many visitors.

'I do get research questions sometimes,' he smiles. 'Some of our members come in to borrow things and occasionally you'll get a reporter doing some sort of story. Some of the members support it because they think they should support it.'

In amongst the old almanacs and videos perhaps the most fascinating artefacts are the library's collection of *American Cricketers*. This periodical was required reading for every Philadelphian player of the time and leafing through its back issues today provides a fascinating insight into the long, slow decline of the game in the city. The editions after World War One are particularly sad. Local match reports dwindle year on year, one by one the prominent Philadelphian clubs become defunct, and the magazine devotes more and more space to players' obituaries and reports of matches abroad. When the *American Cricketer* closes in 1929 it marks the end of an era.

Yet at Haverford the cricketing flame was kept alive by men such as Howard Comfort, a graduate of the college who perhaps more than anyone represents the link between the pre-war era and the revival of the game since the 1970s. Comfort captained the side in 1924 when they won the Halifax Cup, the competition competed for by Philadelphia's foremost clubs and a number of their East Coast rivals which ran annually from 1880 to 1926.

Comfort returned to the college in 1953 and coached the Haverford team for the next three decades, finally handing over to the present incumbent Kamran Khan in the early 1980s. 'Down the years there were many prophecies that baseball would eventually kill off cricket at Haverford, but these were all proved false,' recalls McDougall. 'Most American cricketers between 1930 and 1980 learned the game at Haverford. Even if the game seemed an anachronism to many at the time, the college's commitment didn't ever seem to waver.'

According to McDougall the college authorities invested heavily into the ethical dimensions of the sport, the idea that it acted as a force for improvement among their students. 'This school is very socially conscious,' he says, emphasising the last two words. 'You look at the library and see the kinds of notes posted on the bulletin board – organisations like Amnesty International. This is a very liberal place.'

Outside it's coming up to lunch, so we adjourn to find out how the match is progressing. Toronto have managed to stretch to 199/8. Despite the long tradition of the game at Haverford, the teams are playing on an artificial wicket, causing the ball to rise, making the bowler bowl a fuller length, and thus making things easier for the batsman. Runs are plentiful. The British Officers are set a target of 200 in 40 overs.

While they're waiting for their turn to bat, we get chatting to the British Officers team. There's Brian, the garrulous expat journalist who regales us with tales from his time as publicity officer at Radio One. Another fellow looks and sounds like the spit of Alan Clark, the one-time Conservative MP. Then there's Alfred Reeves, the honorary president, a guy in his 70s who rekindled the club in the 1960s after it had lain dormant for over 40 years.

Though he left Britain nearly two decades previously, Alfred retains the bluff no-nonsense front of a Yorkshireman. He explains how he came to play cricket again in America when he chose a job offer in Philadelphia over one in Seattle.

'Quite by chance my wife and I got an apartment overlooking the Merion ground. I wandered down and noticed that it said "cricket club" on the gates. Well, I wandered up to the gates and waited for someone to come over and say hello. Eventually someone did. So, I said to them "I notice that you play cricket here", and they said, "Well, we used to."

'A few days later I was in our apartment when I said to Betty, my wife, [all excitedly] "I can hear a bat and ball, I can hear it!" I put on my whites and climbed over the wall of this apartment, and I could see some people knocking a ball around. I said, "Do you mind if I join in?" I saw this chap running up to the pavilion and shortly after he left with a guy with a striped blazer and straw hat, bow tie. He came up to me and asked, "Do you bat?" So, I said "Yes, shall I put my pads on?" I put my pads on and batted for them that day. At the end of the match, the captain and the secretary asked, "Would you join us for dinner tonight?" ""Of course, I'd love to, I say. I was in heaven! At one point someone stood up and said, "We have a new member and he is here now, he climbed a wall and made a few runs today and he'd like to speak." So of course I had to stand up then, didn't I?'

Alfred started playing regularly for the Merion team. But as this meant playing only eight or nine games each summer, this proved to be a frustrating experience for a cricket fanatic such as he. At the end of his third season one of his team-mates made a suggestion. 'They didn't seem to get many people and well I said you won't until you start playing more and encouraging people to come along. Then this one fellow Peter Staunton said, "Alfred you're frustrated, I'm frustrated. Why don't we start a team?" "How would we do it?" I asked. "Well, I've been digging around and there was a British Officers team going back to 1875. It died out in 1939 when the war started. Why don't we see if we can get the ground back?" So, he went and bowed to all the right people.'

The right people included the trustees of Haverford and thus the British Officers found their home here. Players were recruited from the expat community and from friends, many of whom had never played cricket before. Alfred simply asked them if they had played tennis before and convinced them that cricket required similar hand-eye co-ordination. These days, he explains, the club floats between 50 and 65 members, mostly expats. 'We have no problem recruiting. A lot of people who come to this country either come on a contract or they come with a big company who easily transfer you around the place. We seem to lose five or six every season and sometimes they are the best players, damn it. But on the other hand, new people always seem to come in.'

While we speak the shadows are lengthening and British Officers are closing in on their target. At six o'clock and with just one over to spare they pass the winning post to the cheers of everyone in the pavilion. Smiles all round. At the presentation both team captains declare that it has been one of those days when cricket was the winner.

British Officers play in a competitive league but there are a clutch of clubs that play what might be termed village cricket, for the sheer love of the game. Three of these clubs are from Philadelphia's illustrious cricketing past and have been revived in recent years to some success.

A few days later we drive to the beauteous surroundings of Chestnut Hill, Northwest Philadelphia and the home of the oldest cricket club in America – Philadelphia CC. It's another gorgeous autumn morning and we're here to meet Tom Culp, the motivating force behind the revival of cricket at the club, and surprisingly, a native-born American.

Philadelphia CC was founded in 1854 in Camden, New Jersey, moving to its present home five or six years later. Tom explains this while presenting us with a book that commemorates the club's 150th anniversary in 2004, a lavish coffee table affair that describes the club's illustrious past, the exploits of JB King (King played for Philadelphia during the final phase of his career), the expansion of the club into tennis, golf and the development of a social scene that would eventually supplant cricket as the club's *raison d'etre*.

For the game stopped being played here in 1922. For over 70 years cricket in any shape or form was wholly absent from the beautifully kept oval we saw that day. The club retained the name merely as a nod to its origins (and probably much to the bemusement of its many guests). Then around the mid-1990s a fellow named Ian Crookenden arrived on the scene.

'He's the director of tennis and he wondered why we weren't playing cricket,' explains Culp. 'I guess there had been an attempt about 10 or 15 years before to revive it and I think there was about half a dozen people who tried to get it going, but there just wasn't the enthusiasm for it. Ian was the driving force within our club. I happened to be in the room that time he proposed it and I remember saying "Well, I don't know how to play but I'll help organise it because I can do that."

'So we just started recruiting people and I mentioned it to my son. He started playing – that was a great drawing card for me because we both learned the sport at the same time. I was over 50 and he was just nine or ten, so it was really great fun in that regard.'

Tom is happy to admit that the newly reconstituted Philadelphia CC were 'terrible, just terrible' at first. 'Batting was a little problematic because we all had baseball swings. We were hitting across the ball instead of curling it. It took us even longer to get the bowling right.' Gradually though they improved and, with the recruitment of a number of Brits, Australians, Indians and Caribbeans, have gained a measure of respectability in their performances.

That is the only thing that matters, for as Tom is keen to point out, the present-day Philadelphians are merely a social cricket club. They are not in a league and because tennis takes precedence during the peak summer months at the club they only play from the beginning of April to mid-May and again from mid-September to the end of October.

Yet the club, playing friendly games against the other Philadelphian teams and sides from New York and Canada, has now been going strong for over a decade. They even managed to go on tour to Argentina where they played as the Gentlemen of Philadelphia, reviving the old touring name their forebears had used all those years ago.

Culp is aware enough to know that the revival is not completely cemented. 'It's really very personality-dependent. By that I mean that I'm willing to do all the grunt work, all the lugging equipment around, ordering it, scheduling matches, etc. I happen to want to do that because I have so much fun playing when we do it. If somebody doesn't want to pick up that mantle – and that could easily happen – then it could easily go away. And you've got to keep finding younger players. We are finding them, but not many. That's a big concern I have. If we had 100 players that would be one thing, but 30 is not too many.'

At the moment the cricket team is 'underneath everyone's radar', he says. 'We're in the club's budget, but it's so small. To use this example: we had a plasma TV stolen out of our bar last week, a very nice TV. Somebody just lifted it off the wall. The price tag for that TV is much higher than the entire cricket budget.'

If the Philadelphia CC budget is small, then the budget at nearby Germantown CC is microscopic. Germantown's story is a remarkably similar one and in fact their motivating force is another genteel American, albeit one with a Caribbean connection.

A white Barbadian who has lived in Philadelphia since the late 70s, we meet Bart Withstandley at the office of the stair company he owns in New Jersey. And he immediately floors us by showing us an antique bat inscribed with what looks like the signature of WG Grace. It seems one of Withstandley's friends found it when he clearing out his loft. 'He showed it to me because he knew I was a cricketer,' he explains. 'I took it home and I saw that there was writing on the back. I cleaned it up, put a magnifying glass on it, looked at it and I saw Grace and I thought, "Holy crap!"

'I went with someone from the CC Morris Cricket Library, their president Paul Hensley. Paul and I looked for books and we found Grace's signature. We looked at Grace's signature with a fellow from England who was the librarian at Lord's. And the three of us looked at the signature and it was identical!'

The bat has apparently been authenticated, and the story is that the great man gave it to a cricketer from Merion, who took it back to Pennsylvania, where it remained long after cricket at Merion ceased in the 1920s.

Withstandley relates this story with an obvious pride. It's an immediate reminder of the Philadelphian cricketing heritage and the links with the English game.

Germantown's story is very similar to Philadelphia's. Both teams were formed within months of each other in 1854 with Germantown moving to its present location in the 1880s. Like Philadelphia, it's a grand setting, a beautiful pavilion that you easily mistake for a provincial English ground, and likewise cricket was revived at the club at roughly the same time in the 1990s. Bart takes up the story:

'About 15 years ago we had a president of the club who said, "I see the name of the place is the Germantown Cricket Club. I suppose we had better play cricket. Is anybody interested?" So a whole bunch of people signed up. We went to a meeting the president called. And he said, "Right, has anyone here actually played cricket?" Two hands went up. One of them was mine and the other one was at the time a 65-year-old Indian. And he said, "Okay you guys can get it organised.'"

So Bart did. And like Philadelphia, Germantown went through an uncomfortable phase of recruiting players, forging themselves as a team and finding their level as a competitive social cricket team with, as Bart describes it, 'no delusions of grandeur'.

Germantown has a regular roster of around 25 players and whilst Bart is adamant that there's no chance of cricket dying out at Germantown again ('at least not while I'm around'), you get the impression that its presence isn't yet secure.

The problem, he says, is the lack of kids playing the game. New players, when they come around, are invariably expats from the cricket-playing nations. None of the Philadelphian teams appear to be breeding a new generation of players, each still being dependent on a steady stream of Asian, Caribbean, English and Australian workers arriving in town and by some stroke of luck locating these reborn clubs.

Most outsiders, in fact most Philadelphians, have little idea that their city supports this urbane oasis where the game from the old country is played much the same as it was one hundred years ago.

You have to wonder too what the other members of these society clubs think of the cricketers who provide their clubs with their names and, to some extent, their history. 'In general, I think everybody at the club appreciates the fact that cricket is still played at the cricket club,' says Bart Withstandley, 'if for no other reason that when people ask them what club they belong to they say, "Oh I belong to the Germantown Cricket Club." And when they ask, "Oh, do they play cricket there?" the member can now respond, "Absolutely!"

'Even if it's nothing more than a curiosity and even if these people have no interest in the game at all they are almost universally interested in the fact that the game is still played there. For them it's a mark of what the old club is supposed to be about.'

Over at Philadelphia the feeling is the same. 'There's not wild enthusiasm,' says Tom Culp. 'Most of them don't understand what's going on but the members of the club who know that we're playing cricket – and most of them at least know that – are highly supportive of the activity just because of the historical significance of it. They think that it's great that we're out doing it.'

How could they not? The sensibilities that pervade these great corridors are much the same as those that the original cricketers had all those years ago: the sense of fair play and sportsmanship that represents cricket and indeed sport at its very best. Once a year this enclave of old-school Philadelphian cricket celebrates these values (and indeed, itself) at an event called the Philadelphia Cricket Festival.

Every May all five clubs – Merion, Germantown, Philadelphia, Haverford and British Officers, plus a number of invited guest teams – play in a round robin tournament that utilises all the grounds round Philadelphia and Haverford. 'You just travel around and play two matches a day,' enthuses Culp, who has a huge smile on his face at the mere mention of the festival. 'It's such fun and we have a social event on at least two of the evenings, a big banquet, usually with a guest of honour. We had Sir Garfield Sobers one time. Gary Kirsten has been here a couple of times.'

The festival was first organised in 1993 as a four-team event but it expanded as the flame of Philadelphian cricket flickered into life once more. Now guest teams come from the UK, Canada and the Caribbean as well as elsewhere in the US and the event is an established part of the Philadelphian social calendar. It's even being marketed as a tourist event where onlookers (and the odd cricket junkie) can imbibe the genteel olde worlde atmosphere.

* * *

The following year, we make our way back to Philadelphia to take in the festival first hand. Rolling up at Merion, we find time to collar Paul Hensley, who apart from being president of the CC Morris library, is also one of the festival's co-organisers.

Hensley has been involved since the festival's early days and has seen the festival grow from a small private affair to one that engrosses the whole neighbourhood and in this particular year, involves 18 teams. 'You know if we took all-comers we'd probably have 30 teams, but we don't have enough pitches for that. At one point Haverford had five pitches on campus and we have sort of tested the waters because we have identified one that could be rehabilitated. Do we want an extra pitch? Don't know. I know we wouldn't have more room at the Merion dinner on Saturday night for a couple more teams. We're just out of space.'

The festival then is at its limit, and though Paul muses about the idea of holding 'qualifying games', you feel that that would run counter to the easy-going beneficent nature of the event. It's organised on a purely voluntary basis. Any money that's made goes to charity – at the time of writing the festival was setting up a fund to support youth cricket.

This year's guest is Shaun Pollock and the South African all-rounder has already been much in demand: 'He's played with quite a few teams this year,' smiles Paul. 'He's

33

a really nice guy and really cool. I was there when he was at Haverford the other night and he was playing with the Haverford kids. He was coaching the kids how to field and giving them advice – I wish I had had that when I was an undergraduate.'

Some of the guests have little idea about the history of Philadelphian cricket and the miniature world the clubs here have created. 'I was showing Garry Sobers around one year as our guest and we walked into the library and he was reading the history and he had this very puzzled look on his face,' remembers Paul. 'Then we jumped in the car and drove over to Merion and walked through the lobby there and we came on to the porch overlooking the field and he just looked at me and said, "You guys are really serious about cricket, aren't you?" And I go "yeah, we really are".

'And it finally sunk in that not only is there this glorious past to tell people about but we have a really great infrastructure that somehow by luck has managed to survive all those years.'

And as Paul speaks we can hear the reassuring sound of leather on willow, punctuated every so often by the peal of church bells. The sun is shining and modern America and all of its problems are far away and everything, at least for a little while, is right with the world.

2

At Home with the Homies

'We went from bullets to balls
from gats to bats
From the streets of concrete
to the grass and mats
We're playing cricket ...'

Theo and Isaac Hayes, 'The Hip Hop Cricket Rap'

TED HAYES is one of those people you notice as soon as they walk in the room. A 6ft 4in middle-aged man with greying dreadlocks and twinkling eyes, he is unlike anybody we've met before. He is also a unique presence within US cricket in that he has attempted to do something unprecedented by building a hub of support for the game in one of the harshest urban environments in the country in South Central Los Angeles.

Many of the people we've met on this journey say that they are on some sort of mission regarding cricket in

America, but no one exudes that missionary zeal quite like Hayes. On our most recent visit to meet him he was on irresistible form. 'We will become known in history,' he says of his team, the Compton Homies and Popz. 'They will read books about us 100 years from now – should the messiah allow it – about how we were the fathers of the revival of US cricket and the revival of global cricket when it becomes the biggest sport in the world, dwarfing soccer and all other sports.'

His is the most unlikely of stories – how a homeless activist caught the cricket bug and ending up travelling round the world with a bunch of street kids, rubbing shoulders with dignitaries from Gerry Adams to Prince Edward, legends like Shane Warne and Brian Lara. But whilst it is Hayes's passion and tenacity in the face of adversity that has pushed down many barriers for his team, we wondered whether that same stubborn streak would see his dreams and hopes for his team ultimately thwarted.

Hayes's background is in street politics. Though he had and indeed still has a finger in a great number of pies, he is probably best known for a project known as Dome Village, a collection of geodesic domes located in the heart of downtown LA. This was set up in 1993 as a kind of halfway community, where homeless men and women gradually learn how to re-integrate themselves into society before moving on to find homes of their own. Hayes, a man who has never strayed far from the front line, had deliberately made himself homeless when he founded a prototype version in 1985, and he both lived and worked in one of the Village's domes from 1993 until the project closed in 2006.

Cricket came into his life through his partner, Katy Haber. An English expat who had worked as production executive on *Blade Runner* and with Sam Peckinpah on several of his movies, Haber knew of a team of Brits working in Hollywood called Beverly Hills CC. When, on a fine day during the summer of 1992, they were a man short for a weekend game, Katy was called to see if she knew anyone who could fill in. Somehow, she persuaded Ted, a man who only knew the word cricket as it related to the insect species, to be the 11th man at the 11th hour.

Ted describes his debut in almost mythical terms. 'I remember they saw me stroll in. This English fellow comes up to me and asks [genteel English accent], "Excuse me, do you bat or do you bowl?" I'm thinking "Bowling? what's that?" I realised later that they thought that I was a West Indian pro who had come to hang out with them for the day.

'So I played the field like a baseball player. They liked my hustle; I got in to bat and actually got six runs that day.

The first time I hit the ball, I did what every American does and dropped the bat and ran to first base.'

Ted was instantly hooked. For him it wasn't just the air of mutual respect that intrigued him but the way the game seemed to hark back to some sort of pre-industrial idyll: 'What it really was about was the etiquette. Hence the whites, indicating a state of purity – the purity of the sport, the purity of the village, what civilisation should be.

'From what I understand real cricket is not the stadium game that is played today trying to look like baseball. Real cricket was a village sport; a social sport designed for fathers and sons to play on the same team together, one village against the other. It was hard competition, but more than that it was the desire to help each other to be better people, at the workplace, at the farm, children towards each other in schools. That is what it was designed for – to civilise and maintain stability in the village.'

A light bulb went off above Ted's head. Why not form a Dome Village cricket team? This could be a vehicle to give the men who passed through its doors a direction, a tool that would help equip them for the challenges they faced re-entering society. Never one to prevaricate when gripped by an idea, Hayes roped in members of the Beverly Hills team and Southern California Cricket Association (SCCA) to start training the team he was calling the Justiceville Krickets.

Corralling a group of homeless men into a functional cricket team would not be easy but Ted had a high profile around LA (he ran for mayor in 1993) and Katy's Hollywood contacts would prove to be invaluable. The Krickets received an early boost when a group of dignitaries representing the business communities of Southampton and Bournemouth passed through Dome Village in 1994. Having heard about the team, they arrived bearing a bat as a gift and a promise that should they ever come over to the UK a game could be arranged at Hambledon. Naturally, Ted took them at their word.

Funded by Prudential Insurance, the Krickets did indeed make it to the game's birthplace and many other English towns the following year. 'I remember we went to Wigan,' Katy recalls. 'You had all these guys wandering around the town centre with the girls in their short miniskirts in the middle of winter and our guys just panting, getting involved with the local bovver boys. I thought, "My God, we'll never get out of this town alive." It was very scary up there.'

The tour not only created something of a media ripple in the UK, it had also raised the men's hopes and spirits. Ted's son, Theo Hayes, could see the difference when the team returned to Dome Village: 'Their eyes had a new glow and a new energy to them. Most of them were like …. "Yeah!" They felt like celebrities. They had been on

TV; people had interviewed them and they felt good about themselves.'

Despite the tour's success Ted and Katy were now presented with a dilemma. 'We realised that cricket and homelessness are not synonymous,' said Katy. 'Homelessness by its very essence is transitory. You can't say, "Don't leave Dome Village and get a job because we want you to stay here and play cricket." People left and the team was disintegrating as soon as we got back.'

It was one of the remaining Krickets, Mustapha Khan, who suggested that Ted and Katy should use what they had learned and take it to Compton. After all, he argued, it's an area where kids are killing each other on the streets. Maybe the message of self-discipline and restraint might find a receptive audience there.

It still seemed a ridiculous notion. Cricket in Compton, the locale known around the world as a byword for crime and violence, the home of gangsta rap? But Ted loved a challenge and was eager to put his ideas into practice. He had a contact on the Compton District School Board and suggested the idea of going into local schools and doing cricket workshops. During spring 1996 this is exactly when Ted and Katy did, culminating in a one-day open-to-all workshop that was attended by the actors Joseph Marcell (Geoffrey from *The Fresh Prince of Bel Air*) and George Lazenby, as well as the Compton Police helicopter.

Among the kids who attended that day were many who made up the core of the team for the next decade and a half – Ricardo and Reuben, as well as Ted's own sons, aspiring rappers Theo and Isaac. Soon people started bringing along their friends and brothers, and a squad gradually developed. In this there were two crucial figures – Ted himself obviously, whose energy was infectious and whose street wisdom won the respect of the young black and Latino kids; but also Leo Magnus, a West Indian coach who had been brought in to teach the young Homies the rudimentary skills of the game.

'Leo was the father of the team,' remembers Ted. 'He taught us how to play the game. He also told us that the umpire is the highest authority on the field. God on Earth, so to speak. If the umpire calls you out you do not eyeball the umpire, you do not question him, argue with him or spit or curse, threaten or hit. No matter how angry you are, you leave the field. He told us the right way to hold the bat, hold our gloves, hold our heads up with dignity, containing your anger, frustrations and feeling of hurt. Then you walk off and take off your gear, put it down in a neat order. Go round the corner until you're out of sight and then freak out, get it out of your system, come back, return to the game and re-focus.'

This is important as many of the young Homies and Popz (the Popz stood for People Of Power) were on the edge of the Compton gang system. Cricket gave them an enjoyable sporting diversion as well as a possible exit route from Compton itself. Ted had high hopes for the team. He saw them as nothing less than the standard bearers of the revival in US cricket. He envisaged the Homies and Popz becoming professionals and touring all over inner-city America, spreading the word about etiquette, respect and self-restraint. But first he needed to establish the team's reputation and make the media sit up and take notice.

In this the team's foreign tours would play a crucial role. The first in 1999 saw a return visit to Hambledon and the towns the Krickets had played in two years previously. It also took in a visit to Ireland that saw the Homies and Popz throw themselves into Britain's own version of inner-city gang warfare.

In 1997 Ted had managed to get the homeless team a tour of the Houses of Parliament through Katy's contacts. As she recalls, there was a large press presence when they arrived at Westminster. 'I remember Ted turned to me and said, "Oh wow, your press release worked, didn't it?" "I don't think it's for us," I replied. It turned out that it was the day that Gerry Adams arrived at the Houses of Parliament to take his seat for Sinn Fein. I pointed out Gerry Adams to him. Ted goes up to Adams, throws his arms round him and greets him. Gerry Adams says, "I don't think I know you. With whom would I be talking?" So, Ted explains about the cricket team and asks, "Why can't we come and play cricket with you in Belfast?"

'Incredibly, he agrees. "Yes, love to. Next time you come to Belfast make sure you call me up." So that sealed it in Ted's head. On the next trip we were going to Belfast.'

That 1999 tour almost didn't happen. The sponsors pulled out at the 11th hour when they got wind that the Homies and Popz would be breaking bread with the Sinn Fein leader. Katy called up one of her UK press contacts and after a sympathetic piece in the *Daily Telegraph*, the publisher Felix Dennis stepped in with the cash to buy the team's shirts, flights and cricket gear.

Over in Belfast word had gone round about the unusual visitors. The team was introduced to Northern Ireland Secretary Mo Mowlam at Stormont whilst negotiations were being conducted with the British government. They presented Gerry Adams with a cricket bat and Ulster Unionist leader David Trimble with a hurling stick. In addition to games against local cricket sides, and in an effort not to appear to be favouring the Loyalists, Ted had arranged for the team to play a hurling match. The homeless activist quite seriously saw the Homies and Popz as international ambassadors of peace and goodwill. 'Our strategy was that if Gerry Adams could take a sport that is hated by the Northern Irish Catholics then it would send a message out to the Catholics, "Hey get off of the guys, let's get above this, it's silly," and send a message to the Brits. "Hey Brits, we are willing to let you know how much I want peace, I am going to handle a cricket bat and ball." And he did it!'

There was also, as Katy explains, an educational dimension to the tour. 'We met the local Member of Parliament there who told us the details about the British–Irish conflict. They loved all that stuff about kneecapping! They were thrilled. I'd never seen them sit so quietly. We wanted them to find out what 800 years of gang-banging can do to a country. And they loved the hotel, The Renshaw, which had a discotheque downstairs. I'd go to bed at night and swear I was sleeping in a drum. If you asked any of them now where in the world they would most like to be they'd say Belfast.'

In between cricket games there were school visits where the team were greeted like visiting superstars. Theo and Isaac would perform their 'Hip Hop Cricket Rap', which extolled, in musical form, the ethics behind the team and the girls would go wild.

'It was like The Beatles all over again,' says Katy. 'There were girls inside the building, girls hanging off the building, girls downstairs … They literally had the clothes taken off their backs by the girls. They lost their hats, their gear, everything. I told them how dangerous Belfast was and when the girls wanted them to walk them home they were terrified. I said, "For God's sake don't wear red or blue!"'

Theo Hayes remembers feeling uneasy too. 'I wasn't comfortable in Ireland at all. But it wasn't the violence – it was because of the lack of black people. It scared the shit out of me. I just wasn't used to going to another country and looking at these dudes who looked like the equivalent of the KKK in my country. I'm not that small a dude but those Irish had some big-assed m*****f*****s – and they looked serious about it.'

The 1999 English and Irish tour was a massive success. Yet whilst it had generated a lot of press in Europe, the US sporting media had largely ignored it. Two years later funds were found for a return visit that took in games in Hambledon, Bristol and finally a game at Windsor Castle (their 1999 fixture there had been rained off). 'I've been in the film business and done a million different things but I never would have gone to Windsor Castle,' reflects Katy. 'And it took a bunch a gang-bangers from Compton to get me there.'

The 2001 tour saw further additions to the Homies and Popz' bulging press file. But it also coincided with 9/11 –

the team's original flight home was on 12 September so they had to return to Bristol and play another game before finally returning to LA the following week. I remember talking to Ted around that time. He was shocked, just like all of us were, but seemed philosophical at the time about the earth-shattering events in New York. 'The darkest hour is always before the dawn,' he quipped.

Yet 9/11 seemed to alter Ted in many ways. On returning to LA he went on a fast, starving himself for several weeks. Even before 2001 his politics were undergoing something of a dramatic shift. Whilst he was protesting at the 2000 Democratic Convention police opened fire on him, injuring him with plastic bullets, but 9/11 accelerated this transformation. He started to become more ostentatiously patriotic and re-orientated himself further towards the neo-conservative right, even courting Republican funders for Dome Village.

He also seemed to become more dogmatic about the team. When two members of the Homies and Popz were invited to England to train with a professional team, Ted vetoed the idea, maintaining that he wanted to keep the team unified as an entity: 'If two or three are singled out and privileged what have we got? We have jockism more than we have the etiquette, which isn't why we came to Compton in the first place.'

Despite his increasing involvement in right-wing politics, with a group of African American Republicans called the Black Elephants and even the anti-immigration neo-vigilante group the Minutemen, Ted was still focused on breaking the Homies and Popz in mainstream America. Hollywood came calling and a number of the major studios made enquiries about the possibility of turning the Homies and Popz tale into a movie. Katy takes up the story.

'Disney bought the rights to the story of the original tour of England in 1995 and Ted and I were very specific about keeping those rights separate. I had led a pretty interesting life before I came to Dome Village. Ted had a very interesting life before Dome Village and lived on the streets for eight years. Neither one of us wanted to give up our life story rights to Disney, so the contract very specifically said, "The life story as it pertains to the homeless cricket tour of England in 1995."

'They hired two writers that did a crappy stereotypical script about smelly homeless people staying at the Savoy, etc. It was really, really corny – a horrible script. They got in another writer and then put the movie into "turnaround". This meant that they weren't going to make it but that someone else could come and pick it up. Of course, no one came and purchased it so it all died.'

'Around 2003 another group of writers started sniffing around the Compton team with a view to making a movie. We said you can as long as it has nothing to do with the rights of the other homeless team and it has nothing to do with the original tour. So they started taking notes and stories from the kids. They took it to New Line, who said they'd love to direct it. Disney came out of the woodwork, saying, "You can't do this unless you pay us $1.3 million in turnaround rights." This is a sequel to the movie that we own because it's about cricket.'

The upshot is that a movie that could have potentially turned Compton's cricketers into household names and given a huge boost to the image of US cricket is still in a state of suspended animation, "development hell" in industry parlance, simply because of the greed of a few people in the Disney corporation.

Whilst these wranglings were going on the team itself was changing. The original squad of 1997 were growing up and finding their own way in the world. Many of them were now fathers, had steady jobs and inevitably found it harder to fit cricket into their busy mature lives. There was also the question of which direction the team should take. On tour they were treated as superstars, but once they returned to Compton it was back to the same old, same old. They didn't even play in a proper league – they competed in the friendly league because Ted didn't want his team to have anything to do with the Southern Californian Cricket Association.

Ted's isolationist stance towards the SCCA dates back to an incident when he and Katy felt the local cricket board snubbed them. 'We offered to do publicity work for them,' insists Ted. 'We felt that if we worked together cricket in America would be huge.'

Katy explains further. 'We offered to help them with a Sri Lankan visit when the 1996 World Cup-winning team came over and it was a disaster. It was a tiny little event. The biggest team in the world at that time was coming to visit LA and Ted and I offered to do the PR, and they turned us down. And it was the biggest non-event. There were more tents than press.'

Whatever the ins and outs of this incident, the result is that the Homies and Popz, arguably the best-known domestic cricket team in America, did not play in a regular league and in all their years of existence played just over 150 games of cricket in total.

Understandably, this lack of regular cricket has led to some frustration within the team. 'I don't want to be seen as a novelty,' Theo Hayes insisted when we met him in 2004. 'I don't want to be nobody's charity man!' Meanwhile, his father is often upset that his charges don't always uphold the high ethical standards he has laid out for them: 'You look at the Homies and Popz and their gear is everywhere,' he rants. 'We are violating cricket, every time we lay down our gear without being aware. It's filled with disrespect to the sport, but most of all it shows we disrespect ourselves.'

And thus Compton Cricket Club remained at an impasse, unable to fulfil the ambitious dreams of its founder and with every possibility that as players grow up and gradually drift away, the team will wither and die. But the Compton experiment has been very far from a failure, as the story of one team member shows.

Ricardo, a Latino kid, was one of the original players who showed up to the 1996 workshop. Though he's far from a stereotypical gang member, Ricardo has had two spells in prison. He was accused of being an accomplice in a drive-by and was looking at a 15-year stretch before Ted and Katy hired a top attorney that managed to reduce his sentence to three years. 'He did a year on probation,' recalls Katy, 'and the final day of probation, they did what they do, which is a probation raid on the house. His father and I believe innocently because his father is a really decent guy and was holding some luggage of a friend of his while the friend was in Mexico. The police did a search and in the luggage was a gun. And Ricardo was taken back to jail for another two years. It had nothing to do with him.'

'And yet he came out and you'd think he had never stopped playing cricket. He is such a fine cricketer. When I organise a game, he's the one to whom I say, "Can you tell everyone." He's come out of jail beautifully. There is such a calmness about him now. He's such a sensitive chap, a really good guy.' Ricardo ended up studying to become, of all things, a cop.

The last time we met Ted Hayes he was still talking the big talk, still full of big plans for the Homies and Popz. The problem, as it had always been, was finance. Despite their contacts and high profiles, Ted and Katy have been unable to attract long-term funding for their project. Their dream of putting the team on a stipend so they can tour the US and spread the word about cricket wasn't ever realised. 'We have promised them so much and we really haven't come through because we haven't had the financial ability,' reflected Katy ruefully.

* * *

For years we heard nothing more from the team. But as we reached the end of our odyssey, we made contact once more and were able to catch up – albeit remotely – with both Katy and Rick Miller, the Homies and Popz' self-styled 'token white guy'.

The team had continued for a while, playing in the friendly league. There was one more tour, to Australia in early 2011. They were financed by a philanthropist/donor named Hugh Snellbrook and were also helped along the way by an aptly named England player. Katy: 'Nick Compton, when he heard about the Australian tour, came over and trained with everybody, before we left.

'We played a seven a side in Napa Valley. Nick was the captain, and we took advantage of him being here. I have this wonderful shirt that he gave me,' she says as she holds up Compton's signed England shirt. But even before the Australia tour there were signs the team were fraying, much of this – according to Rick at least – as a result of Ted's right-wing politics.

'He went on the radio around the time of the Obama presidency, laying into Obama and at that time there was a lot of tension between him and Theo. Theo to his credit said, "No, me and the rest of the team are actually fine with Obama."

'I do remember Raul turning down the Australia trip, saying, "I've got my values, I respect Ted – he's done a lot for me – but I just can't agree with him on his politics. I'm not against him. But I'm not going to go with him, either." Raul was by far the most mature out of any of us about it.

'Everyone was excited to be in Australia, but it did fall apart whilst on the tour. There was tension between Ted and Theo, tension between Ted and the rest of the group and then there was tension between Theo and the rest of the group.

'When he [Ted] spoke to the media on that tour, he would speak about those kind of things – mostly immigration. He was already aligned with that whole "build a wall" thing. That was one of the points he and Theo clashed on. Theo also spoke to the media and would say, "Oh, he (Ted) doesn't speak for us."

'The Ted–Theo thing was father/son rivalry, a lot of abandonment issues. And then Theo was drinking. He pretty much disappeared at one point. We didn't know where he was. He was on a drinking binge, he would end up with some girl. We didn't see him during the last half week of the tour, until he showed up drunk at the airport.'

In the midst of all this Ted quit, at least temporarily. 'He wanted the team to apologise to him for his son's behaviour. Or he wanted his son to apologise to him for the team's behaviour. He had some demands and I think Katy talked him down and he rejoined us after a few days.

'There was a bit of a power-sharing agreement, where Theo and Emilio were both team captains and had different ideas of how to do things. One of the anger points for Ted was that Theo took him out of bowling because Ted had given away way too many runs and he did it in front of the rest of the team. Ted said, "That's bunk, I'm not doing this anymore." And then I remember back at the hotel Ted wouldn't even come out of his room. He took to drinking wine. Theo took to drinking beer.'

Asked about her experiences of the tour, Katy simply says: 'I really don't want to talk about it.' Clearly, it was that painful. 'It was basically the collapse of the team. It wasn't something that I could see coming.'

The Homies and Popz played one more season in the friendly league but things began to wind down after that. By 2013 they were playing just occasional games with visiting sides. The team website is still online, but has not been updated since 2015.

So were Ted's politics a factor in their demise? 'Absolutely not,' Katy fires back. 'It was time. It was time for it to go in a different direction. I think Ted was disappointed, but you know he had to get on with his life as well.'

'My own personal view is that they were a victim of their success,' says Rick. 'They got these kids through some rough years and everyone just became an adult and became busy and couldn't really commit in the same way. They had jobs. Some of them had kids. People had moved on. And Katy and Ted just didn't have the energy or ability to continue to pull in new people.' Mustapha Khan, who had taken cricket to Compton with Ted and Katy in the first place, still runs a cricket programme in Compton.

The Compton Homies and Popz didn't spearhead the revival of the sport in the US in the way Ted originally envisaged. But in human terms, the team achieved all its objectives and more. By taking these young men under their wings at a crucial time in their upbringing, Ted and Katy used cricket to make a positive difference to these young men's lives, men who might otherwise have ended up on drugs, dead or in prison. It's just a pity that to this day so many Americans remain unaware of their achievements.

But the story, or at least the story of the story, is not quite over. Katy is currently working on the Homies and Popz film, though she's cagey about what stage the project is at. 'The timing feels right,' she says. Cricket is now confirmed to be part of the Los Angeles Olympics in 2028. The Homies and Popz may yet be immortalised on the silver screen, which will be a deserved testament to the vision of two incredible people. And the life-changing qualities of cricket.

Clifford Severn

The figure that connects the Homies and Popz to the pre-war era of Californian cricket was an old man whose life in cricket encompassed that of a player, administrator, groundsman, sustainer and supporter. We met him at a Homies game in 2004.

He was 79, but looked much older; like an Old Testament prophet, a living portal to an increasingly distant time.

Severn was born in London in 1925, but at the age of eight his family moved to California. There, Clifford found success as a child actor, appearing in a number of Hollywood films including *A Christmas Carol* and *How Green Was My Valley*. Alongside his father, he also began to play for the Hollywood Cricket Club.

'I am the only surviving member,' he told us. 'I first played when I was eight years old. I was always begging that the team would show up short so I would get a chance to play. We had Brits who were writers, directors, actors and agents, everybody who was involved in the movie industry and of course Sir Aubrey Smith who was one of the icons, who always played a typically British character. Then there was David Niven and my favourite name for him was "Hat Trick", because he got a hat-trick against some visiting San Francisco guys. Basil Rathbone, Errol Flynn and a tremendous number of character actors played.'

Together with his father, Clifford kept cricket going in California throughout the war years when a lack of personnel could have easily seen it die. He went on to represent the US national team, making his debut at the age of 39. Before then he had found time to pay homage to one of the greatest American players of them all: John Bart King.

'I heard that he was not well and getting along in years and I was told he was at this hospital and I just made it my business to show up. I showed up with a ball and a cricket bat and we had a lovely discussion about some of his exploits. For me it was absolutely thrilling. I should it put in the same light as if I was lucky enough to have met Don Bradman.

'I was too young to see him play. But my dad had always waxed poetically about the guy and anybody who you ever spoke to, when it comes up for discussion about who is the best American cricketer that ever was JB King's name would come up. And for good reasons. He was universally recognised as being just so far, head and shoulders above everyone. Bowler par excellence. Marvellous batsman and naturally an excellent fielder.'

When we met him, Severn was still playing occasionally for his pub team. He suffered a stroke in 2010 but didn't put down his bat until the following year. He died in June 2014 at the age of 88. These days the phrase 'legend' is overused to the point of banality, but if anyone can claim to have played a legendary role in Californian cricket, or indeed resembled a legend, it was Clifford Severn.

3

The New York Underground

IT IS both emblematic and exceptional. Close your eyes, think of America and images associated with the city intrude upon your imagination. Yet, like most 'world' cities, it stands apart, indeed frequently in opposition to the nation's perccived 'heartland'. New York might act as a magnet, but it repels as well as attracts.

In cricketing terms New York remains – like the country as a whole – brimming with potential yet unable to capitalise on it. The city is arguably the sport's strongest US outpost and is home to more cricketers than any other part of the country, but is divided, disorganised and, due of its sheer scale, unable to organise itself into the driving force and the engine the US game has long needed.

Cricket has had a continuous presence here for well over a century and a half. Every summer weekend you can, if you so wish, take a journey out of Manhattan and visit where

New York City 'begins' (as the sign that greets you on the Brooklyn side of Manhattan Bridge insists). Venture further and you'll discover the playing fields of Brooklyn, Queens and the Bronx – Van Cortlandt Park, Canarsie, Gateway, Marine Park, Floyd Bennett and Baisley Point. There you'll hear the shouts, the appeals, the clangour of cricket New York-style – a game that has taken on the characteristics of this exhilarating city, a subcultural community that most of its US-born white residents are still barely aware of.

We say 'still', since at the end of the Noughties that community briefly poked its head above the cultural parapet when novelist Joseph O'Neill used it as the backdrop to his 2008 novel *Netherland*. His narrator Hans is a Dutchman who, separated from his family after they flee the city post-9/11, takes succour playing cricket and making friends among its marginalised milieu. *Netherland* was a huge critical success and at least posited the idea into the cultural and sporting ether that New York could be, and maybe already is, a cricketing city. As much as Sydney, Bridgetown or Lahore.

It is this dream, that the city could be the propellant behind the revival of the game in America, that has fired its players, administrators and entrepreneurs for a generation. The dream has attracted its fair share of hucksters – indeed one of *Netherland*'s main characters is a shady cricket entrepreneur named Chuck Ramkissoon – but perhaps those are better discussed in another chapter. Our mission for the moment is to trace the contours of the game here, a game that has been shaped, more than most US cities, by immigration.

* * *

For many American cricketers have started their careers and their journey here (though their first sight of the US these days is more likely to be the tarmac at JFK rather than the Statue of Liberty, as was the case a century back). It was immigration – largely from the Caribbean – that kept the game alive during the inter-war years after it had gasped its last virtually everywhere else in the US. But whilst the game was still visible during its final days in Philadelphia, in New York cricket went underground, undetected and unrecorded by the mainstream US media. It benefited immensely from the huge strides West Indies cricket made during those years. As the game in the islands developed and migration north – particularly to Boston and New York – continued throughout the first half of the 20th century, it had a knock-on effect on the game in the North East. New teams, consisting wholly of Caribbean immigrants formed and existing teams were refreshed and often transformed by these new Americans.

One such was Staten Island CC. Formed in 1872 by expat members of the British Armed Forces, they hold the accolade of being the longest-running continuously playing cricket club in the United States, with Walker Park, their home since 1886, the longest continuously used ground. It's here, at this slightly gone-to-seed municipal facility just a stone's throw from the Staten Island Ferry, where we meet Clarence Modeste, an elderly West Indian gentleman who has been involved with the club for over 50 years.

Clarence is now 93 and has lived a remarkable life. A Tobagan, he lived in the UK where he attended Eton as a child. 'Back then there were lots of Caribbean people who came to the US,' he recalls. 'Mainly they came as itinerant labourers, farm labourers – they came in autumn to pick the apple crop. Mostly they came on short-term visas for three months, four months. They would work, make some money, go back home and then they would come back next year.'

It was inevitable this would impact on sport. 'During the 1930s, in the third world countries there was much worse poverty than in first world countries – even though things were really bad here. One solution was to get one or two of your children off to the United States, where they could find some sort of job, and it was between the 1930s and 1940s that more West Indians started coming to places like New York, settling down and starting to play cricket.'

The revival of the game in the US began here, although as Modeste notes, tracing this revival is difficult as so few of the clubs kept records back then. Staten Island CC itself has a gaping hole in its history – a fire at its clubhouse in 1932 destroyed many records. Even now its website does not even bother to mention the revival in cricket during the 1940s and 50s.

Staten Island play in the Metropolitan League, which itself is the longest continuously running cricket league in the US. It dates back all the way to 1879, just two years after the first Test between England and Australia and has managed to keep the flag flying for US cricket even during its lowest points. Its history and survival is an obvious source of pride for secretary Sham Ali.

We met Ali in 2014, at a cafe in mid-town Manhattan, just around the corner from his workplace. Born in Guyana, he's lived in the city since 1977, around the same time he and his friends formed the Cosmos team. Though initially a predominantly Guyanese side, he believes both he and they have absorbed their adoptive city's fire and resolve: 'In New York City, we are aggressive people. We say and do what we want to say and do and tend to take some of that out on to the cricket field. We are not very laid back. But you have to have that inner fight in you to perform and do well. New York teaches us that – to keep pushing forward to get things done.'

The city's cricket community has had to draw on those reserves of grit and determination to get, well, anything done. In recent years much of the battling has been directed into trying to find new grounds and preserve existing ones. At present there are just 16 cricket facilities in the whole of the five boroughs, and even on those cricket is having to compete with baseball and soccer – both more established sports – for time and space. You can see how it could wear a man like Ali down. He details the woes that have recently gone on at Floyd Bennett, a disused aerodrome near JFK airport that has been a federally owned sports facility for decades. Having used the facility since 1980, Cosmos have recently been presented with a significantly increased bill to use it next season.

Even putting aside ground difficulties, things are hard going, he explains. The Metropolitan League has recently reverted to one division as a couple of teams have dropped out. Trying to keep up with the website is difficult too – at the time of writing it hadn't been updated since 2011. The same problems are affecting all the other leagues within the New York metropolitan area.

'For the most part it's two things – financial struggles and the stability of teams,' he reflects. 'Many teams operate with one or two people doing the bulk of the work and don't have a place where they can gather and get business done.

It's usually done in the basements of one of the guys' houses. Teams survive as a result of one or two people funding the process. I mean it costs us around $5,000–$6,000 a season to play. That's a lot of money. It works out to be maybe $300 a member, if you have about 15 members.'

Then there is the lack of young players to pick up the reins from their elders. 'I have been in the Metropolitan League since 1983 and it's the same guys and we have all gotten old. We play masters now and there is not an influx of new people. The youths who are playing cricket in the schools, they do not have the club experience. The people who play in the Metropolitan League and the other leagues were mostly from the Caribbean and we came to the US with a background of club experience. We all knew what it meant to be part of a club. The youths now, they don't. We try and sit them down and talk about the club but they seem lost. When we say, "We need to have a meeting" or "You need to be part and parcel of the club" or "You guys have to put out the matting, the water, come and help us" … well, they don't seem to have that awareness.'

But at least the Metropolitan League is still there. 'The Nassau League hasn't played for a couple of years,' Ali points out. 'They are pretty much defunct. The Brooklyn and American cricket leagues – their average age is rising. There is not an influx of youth joining them. The others

– us, the Eastern American and Commonwealth – are holding up okay.'

Any progress in improving general playing standards is hampered by the Balkanised nature of the scene – the Metropolitan features mostly players and clubs of Jamaican origin plus some from the other Caribbean islands, the Eastern American is predominantly Guyanese, the American League Bajan, the Brooklyn League Asian with a scattering of Caribbean teams. The Bangladeshi League, as the name suggests, Bangladeshi. The obvious thing to do would be to merge all six to create a combined greater New York league, a pyramid system that would allow the cream to rise to the top (and make national team selectors' lives considerably easier). That, though, would require existing administrators to give up a large portion of their current power and influence – and their own standing within their communities – for the greater good of the game.

Turkeys voting for Christmas, in other words. 'Leagues do not want to give up their territory,' says Ali. 'That has been the main stumbling block over the years and we just cannot get it over it. I have written about it and suggested it myself. Some people agreed that it would be a good idea but nothing more happened. It has to happen for the betterment of the cricket. If it doesn't, we are not going to survive another ten years.'

Ali's despondency is shared by another league president we meet a few days later. Like his Metropolitan League counterpart Lesly Lowe has given the best part of his life to New York cricket. Incredibly, he has been the president of the Commonwealth League since its inception in 1979 (it's the youngest of the six New York leagues). A large, imposing man, Guyanese by origin, Lowe is courteous and again, obviously proud of the fiefdom he had built up in those three decades. We meet him in a bar up in the Bronx, a stone's throw away from Van Cortlandt Park, the municipal facility where the Commonwealth League play their games every weekend of the summer.

Of all the league presidents Lowe is probably the one who has most reason to feel confident. His organisation has nearly 100 teams and by far the most players. Indeed, there are more Commonwealth League players than all the other five leagues combined. Their age profile is altogether healthier too – 75% of Commonwealth League teams are comprised of players between the ages of 18 and 25. Yet despite this Lowe too seems forlorn about the state of cricket in his city.

'I've been around cricket for so long and each year you hear promises made by many different people and promises made by this organisation, that organisation, promises made by USACA, promises made by ICC. Nothing. Ever.

Materialises. Nothing significant ever happens. I'm not optimistic that in the next few years there'll be cricket stadiums, and we'll have one-day internationals. I don't see that happening. Americans are not catching on to the game. They are not interested, period. I see only expatriates keeping the game alive.'

He too doesn't think the idea of a pyramid league structure will be put into practice any time soon. 'I think it's a good idea, but I guess each league still likes their independence. Someone has to make the first move. If everyone is holding back, you know, "Let's see what this guy is going to do" ...' he lets the words fade away. The implication is there.

* * *

We come away from our meetings with Ali and Lowe feeling despondent ourselves. Both men have given the best part of their lives to nurturing the game in New York, but neither seems to have much to show for it. They seem ground down by their efforts, displaying a mixture of bruised entitlement that their work has received so little payback and frustration that no one else has arrived to relieve them of their burden. The unanswered question is what will happen once this generation of ageing Caribbean administrators finally pass on? Will New York cricket be left to wither and die?

If there is hope it resides in two projects that have emerged over the last decade. Crucially, both originated from outside the existing US cricket community.

Last decade the city's education department, sensing that cricket was a growing sport, decided to add it to its roster of league sports, alongside basketball, American football, baseball and soccer. Indeed, it was whilst journeying around the five boroughs that the chief executive of School Support Services, a white middle-aged New Yorker called Eric Goldstein, first encountered the sport, its strange rituals and idiosyncrasies. It piqued his interest.

'In parts of Queens, the Bronx and Brooklyn but particularly Queens on weekends you'll see men playing cricket, in their whites,' he explains. 'I'd be travelling around these places, see these guys and I'd say to Donald (Douglas, the executive director of the Public Schools Athletics League or PSAL) "Probably these are working guys. They're working all week and on the weekends they're playing cricket." So we said, "I bet you there are kids behind them. But these guys are not letting them play because it's their time."

'The other thing that's really interesting now is that 60, 70 years ago these kids came to America, the process of the Americanisation would be really strong. My father and my grandfather's generation, you forgot the old country, you had to grow up the American way. You played baseball, you played football. That doesn't exist anymore. People travel back and forth. They have satellite TV from wherever they are. And on demand they can watch cricket. People take this for granted. That connection to wherever they are from is still very strong. And if where they are from cricket is in their mother's milk, they are staying with it. So that is a big part of this too – a big part.'

To become part of the PSAL curriculum a sport has to fit a number of criteria. Most obviously it has to encourage physical activity amongst schoolchildren. But there also has to be some sort of critical mass – enough kids to form at least four to eight teams and 'growth potential' in terms of the sport's profile and numbers of kids playing.

Cricket ticked all these boxes and so Goldstein trialled the concept, organising a one-day tournament at Gateway in Brooklyn. Scores of kids turned up and the day was considered enough of a success for the league to get green-lighted. The first public schools cricket league in the US has been an enormous success and at last count had 30 competing schools.

The next day we wend our way over to Newcomers School on the north-easternmost tip of Brooklyn. It's appropriately named, as the majority of its yearly intake are just that – immigrants fresh off the plane from Asia and Africa. Incredibly though, their cricket coach isn't an Indian or Caribbean American but a white woman from the Bronx who until two years ago knew next to nothing about the sport.

Christine Cavaliere sits back in a chair in her school foyer and beams. Unlike the others we've interviewed thus far during our New York sojourn she is brimming over with enthusiasm and zest for the game she barely knew anything about until recently. 'The boys have always played it out in the school yard. So for the five years I've been teaching at Newcomers, I would go outside and watch them play in the school yard. I'd talk to the boys – "how do you play?" and "what's going on?"

"Then my assistant principal got word from Donald Douglas that they were starting a cricket league. So I put a piece of paper up on the notice board in the gym. "Anyone interested in playing cricket for the school, write your name." That was in the morning. By 12 noon I had a list of 45 names.

'So I knew that this was something that we're going to do. I typed in "cricket" into the internet and saw what came up – there was the Laws of Cricket. I started refreshing myself on all the things I saw on the BBC, what I saw in the school yard and put it all together.

'Then I went outside and I played with the boys. The boys were all, "Miss, we don't want you to get hurt." You know, the ball comes fast. So they took it easy on me at first. But I learned through them. A lot of the time when you have lunch guys come up to the office and they talk about cricket. And they were just as happy to give up any free time they had to help me and help each other and do what they love. And cricket is what they love. And I love cricket now myself. Yeah definitely, definitely!'

Cavaliere dropped into Singh's Sporting Goods in Brooklyn (New York's premier outlet for cricket equipment), bought all their gear, videos about the sport and started learning on the job. She took what she already knew from coaching baseball and adapted it to the new sport. Luckily, her charges were pretty good raw material as most came from Pakistani, Afghani or Bangladeshi backgrounds. In their first season they ended up as league champions, winning ten matches and losing just two.

'In the beginning I felt I was a little over my head,' she admits. 'But I love sports, and I love my kids. Their enthusiasm put any doubt I had out of my mind. They were confident and I was confident. You know, "We can do this." There are fundamental coaching principles that carry over into any sport – hard work, determination, sportsmanship. And those took us all the way into the finals at the end.'

The team's success had a ripple effect inside the school. 'Other cultures have got into it too! When we were outside playing at the school some of the Dominican or Chinese students who usually play basketball, now they're stopping and watching. "Hey, why's this guy taking 30 paces out and running full speed ahead and bowling this ball? What's he doing? What's going on?" They hear the crack of the ball on the bat and they love it. Polish students come and go "Miss, what's going on? Wow, look at that! That guy can really bat. Wow! Look how fast he's throwing that ball! Look how fast he's pitching!" I'm like "Ah, now you can learn some vocabulary – it's called bowling."'

As the first public schools cricket league in the country, Eric Goldstein is justifiably proud of the project. 'We have 350 high schools in New York City. The state of Ohio, I don't think, has 350 high schools! So just to put it in scale, we have a little over a million schoolchildren in New York City. The operating budget for New York City public schools per annum is $17 billion. It's a big, big place. So to do it on this type of scale is significant. Now we've shown that it can work I wouldn't be surprised if other districts get around to it.'

But the PSAL league isn't the only initiative that is happening in New York. The NYPD set up their own league for kids between the ages of 14 and 19 in 2008. However, unlike the schools board, the police department appear a lot less eager to talk about their baby. We leave messages and attempt to contact the officials in charge of the project and even set up one interview, only for it to be cancelled at the last moment.

Eventually after we leave town the best we can get is an email conversation with Sgt Adeel Rana, the main organiser for the 2013 season. 'The league has given hundreds of NYC youth a great healthy activity to occupy them during the summer,' he suggests. 'It's provided them with a great opportunity to compete, a great feeling of self-confidence and accomplishment in an environment which promotes practice, teamwork and hard work. It's also provided an excellent environment for police and youth interaction with a new immigrant youth community that previously did not have many similar interactions.'

This last point would appear to be one of the main motivating forces behind the project – the idea being that as South Asian (in particular Pakistani, Afghani and Bangladeshi) kids make up the majority of the young cricket-playing population in New York, getting them involved in a project like this proves an excellent way to improve community relations. Indeed, this was confirmed in a BBC interview with the then organiser Amin Kosseim in 2011. 'We have so many different communities in New York but we didn't have a specific outreach with the South Asian community. Yes, we had a rapport with them. But we wanted a better rapport with them.'

***

Our time in New York is almost up but we have one last person to meet – a figure who has done more to alert the world to the New York cricket scene than any administrator, official or entrepreneur. We arrive at his apartment at the Chelsea Hotel, the iconic mid-town establishment famous in the 20th century for its artistic bohemian clientele – Dylan Thomas, Jack Kerouac, Joni Mitchell, Leonard Cohen. Joseph O'Neill is in distinguished company. *Netherland* was one of those rare literary novels that gets talked about, has broadsheet and *Newsweek* features written about them. All the more remarkable then that it's set amongst the dreamers of the beleaguered New York cricket scene.

It was also heavily autobiographical. Like O'Neill, the lead character Hans is a white European playing cricket in a city where the sport is almost entirely the preserve of Caribbean and Asian immigrants. 'The idea was to write about cricket, because it is a news story. It felt like news,' he explains. 'It felt like something that I knew about and nobody else knew about. I suppose as a novelist you have to try and write about your obsessions, if you can. And for me cricket certainly falls into that category.'

O'Neill himself plays for Staten Island CC and has encountered many of the same people we've met on the New York scene. Indeed, one meeting we have with the

Cricket Promoters Association is strikingly similar to that which Hans has with Chuck Ramkissoon, a hustling cricket entrepreneur who dreams of building a cricket stadium on Floyd Bennett Field (see chapter 6). Does he, like Hans learns to in the book, now play it as an American, as a New Yorker?

'Ha, I'm just glad to just stand up! I'll play as any nationality. But yes, here because of the state of the pitches your shots just go away. I open the batting and after about eight or nine overs, well, you've just got to get on with it. There's just no way you're going to bat on and find yourself 112 not out at the end of the day. You can't do that. It's death or glory. And also, half the guys I'm with can't run between the wickets. In fact, they can barely run at all.'

Netherland wasn't an easy sell. 'Everyone said "why on earth?" I spent years writing this book and no one was interested, and everyone would be saying, "Why are you writing about such an absurd, tiny, marginal part of the culture?" In the end there was only one editor who was interested and even then it took a long time for a small amount of money. But luckily for me the boss of Random House was an Indian and he loved it, gave it a little push and for some reason it was read by … well, I think there was some genuine word of mouth going round.'

That's an understatement. When news came that even President Obama had read the book, O'Neill knew he had created a genuine sensation. Part of its success was timing, he suggests. *Netherland* tapped into a post-War On Terror mood that sought to look afresh at how the US relates to and engages with the rest of the world.

'I just think I was lucky,' he reflects. 'The thing about cricket is that it's asking Americans to think about a narrative which isn't their own. That was part of the initial project of the book and cricket was a kind of metaphor for all that. But then in a way I was fortunate because during the Bush years people got fed up. When the book came out, they were ready to hear a new story. That kind of extremely narrow insular definition of Americanness which was adopted by the Bush administration – which was also disastrous – was something that had ran its course. They were thirsty for something new.'

This idea of America – after a period of bruised introspection – now being ready to learn something from the rest of the world is one of the themes of the book. One of the most striking passages of *Netherland* is where Chuck Ramkissoon explains about the moral and ethical dimension of the sport and decides that countries cannot call themselves civilised until they've embraced the game of cricket. Does the author agree with that?

'I don't have any views on that,' O'Neill blocks. 'I do think though that there's a basic validity to the question how does the US expect to understand the world if it can't understand something as simple as cricket, which is an obsession for large parts of the Muslim world? This is what Chuck is saying – the USA has to have connections to the Muslim world. It's not going to connect with them on a religious level. It's not going to connect on any other level. Why not sport, the great connector?

'I mean, you learn about the world through sport. When I was a boy how did I hear about Budapest? How did I hear about Rio de Janeiro? And Chuck has the same thing – he learns about Birmingham and places like this on his radio. Sport has always been a force for cultural understanding and the displacement of tribal composition. It's never clear from Chuck how opportunistic his ideological interests are, but I think his basic point is a good one. In fact there have been articles in the *New York Times* saying that Americans should learn how to play cricket.'

In the short term this seems unlikely. What's clear though from our time in New York is that the sport here has only made strides forward when native-born Americans have taken it up. 'To progress it has to get over this immigrant sport niche,' O'Neill argues. 'I mean that is what Chuck is trying to do. His narrative is that it's an ancient sport in America and, if you think of it as an immigrant hobby, then you're never going to get anywhere.'

If O'Neill sees hope it is with the South Asian community. 'That generation of Caribbeans haven't been able to transform it economically. Whereas the Indians might. It might happen with a greater economic power and that … cultural confidence. I think there's a kind of entrepreneurial tradition in Indian immigrant patterns that could be translated into sporting entrepreneurship, and I also think that most West Indians are black and I don't think it's the best starting point in the world if you're trying to start a business in the United States.'

It's a contentious, depressing way to end our meeting before we descend the Chelsea's spiral staircase and wend our way out on to the streets, out of the city, still musing on what we've heard during the last few days. Cricket here remains stuck between its past and future. For all their good work the likes of Sham Ali and Lesly Lowe represent New York cricket's venerable Caribbean past. Christine Cavaliere's kids embody its future. And if those kids grow up, integrate and become Americans – cricket-playing Americans – then maybe the New York scene, with the huge natural advantages it possesses – a critical mass of players, a constant influx of young cricketers plus that abundance of grit, aggression and determination – may yet provide US cricket with the jump start it so badly needs.

The Cricket Hall of Fame

After New York we head northwards. It's a two-hour drive out of the city, through the dark to Hartford, Connecticut where we meet the men and women behind the Cricket Hall of Fame.

It must be said, the concept of a sporting hall of fame is very American. In the UK we tend not to bother with such things, perhaps shying away from the back-slapping self-congratulatory aspect of it all. The idea certainly hasn't caught on in English county cricket or Premier League soccer. Not yet, anyway. But there's a Baseball Hall of Fame and an American Football Hall of Fame, so why not one for cricket too?

That was the original thinking behind it, says Pauline Davis, one of the project's organisers. 'We started in 1980. Nobody else was doing it, so why not us?' She explains how cricket grew in the Hartford area, how Caribbean farm workers gravitated to the local area in the 1930s and 40s and began playing cricket. A social club was started, which is where the hall of fame still resides.

Her colleague Ovid John is keen to point out that the hall of fame is not just related to US cricket, but the game in general. 'It was to recognise international players. We wrote to the West Indies board of control and got their information and then wrote to the individuals and sent them an invitation – our first inductees were Lance Gibbs of Guyana and Alfred Valentine of Jamaica. We have had some big names over the years – Clive Lloyd, Sir Garfield Sobers, Greg Chappell – he was going to come but fell ill so we had to do it via video conferencing.

'Most of these guys were really receptive,' he says. 'Because at that time there was no other hall of fame anywhere else. We have more of a struggle now because since then all of these other countries are coming up with their own thing and they have more money than we do because they are a bigger cricket-playing country. We have no funding.'

There are no great and good, or famous names on the committee. 'You're looking at the committee right here. It's just the credibility that's keeping us going, because we've been here for 25 years, we have more credibility than all these other ones.'

The group said they were looking for sponsorship and talked about their hopes of creating a cricket museum at the club, which as of 2024 is still a possibility. Since then they have inducted a long list of cricket's great and good, including many who have made significant contributions to the game in the US. Roy Sweeney from the Promoters Association was inducted in 1991, Homies and Popz coach Leo Magnus in 2004. Lesly Lowe from New York's Commonwealth League was inducted in 2009, John Aaron in 2012 and coach and trainer Basil Butcher Jr in 2019. And the hall of fame honoured the grand old man of New York cricket Clarence Modeste with a Lifetime Achievement Award in 2023.

Perhaps it is these local inductees that are most significant. Test-playing legends of the game hardly need an extra gong on their mantelpiece, but US cricket is not short of unheralded heroes whose decades of hard graft in the shadows fully deserve to be recognised.

4

The Cricket Junkies

The Decline and Fall of USACA

Each man kills the thing he loves,
By each let this be heard,
Some do it with a bitter look,
Some with a flattering word,
The coward does it with a kiss,
The brave man with a sword!'

Oscar Wilde, from the *Ballad of Reading Gaol*

THE UNITED States were one of the three nations to be admitted to the ICC as Associate members as part of the organisation's general shake-up in 1965. But whilst Sri Lanka – who were also admitted at the same time – have gone on to become an undoubted force in world cricket, even winning a World Cup in 1996, the US's journey has not been as smooth. Arguably it's been in a state of long-term arrested development.

How much of that is due to the inadequacies of its governing body? The United States of America Cricket Association (USACA for short) was formed in 1961 and though its initial driving force John Marder was highly regarded enough to be made a life member of MCC, by the early 2000s its reputation had plummeted and then some.

Sports administration and sports administrators don't have a great reputation at the best of times, but barely anyone we encountered during our years researching this tale has had a good word to say about USACA. The strength of feeling has ranged from laughing dismissal to the potentially libellous. The charges are that they are guilty of incompetence, negligence and corruption and are a group of amateurs fumbling around, unable to provide the funding, drive and vision necessary to take the game forward in the US.

Virtually the first person we met on this odyssey, Clarence Modeste in New York, rolled his eyes at the mention of USACA: 'They exist. Heaven knows why. They don't think of anything and if they don't want to do something they stand in the way of anyone else doing it.'

At that time, October 2004, the governance of US cricket was in a state of flux. On one hand there was a fair amount of hope. It looked like the ICC were going to get their hands dirty and make a concerted effort to develop the Stateside game. They had announced an initiative called Project USA and appointed British sports development bod Gary Hopkins as its chief executive. The idea was simple – Hopkins would leverage his contacts and experience to stage one-day internationals and bring the best teams in the world to the US. The ensuing funds would be put back into the development of grassroots cricket in America.

In an interview with *Cricinfo* in September 2004, Hopkins talked about visiting '10 to 12 locations' with an eye to finding suitable venues to stage such events. 'I'm very heartened by what I've seen,' he said. 'With a bit of understanding and a bit of creativity we can create a true cricket environment. It may not be an environment you see at Lord's, but it will be a great wicket and a great outfield, and I believe we're on the way to finding these sorts of locations.'

Project USA was very much a top-down affair – in effect the ICC were trying to bypass USACA, who at that time were once more teetering on the verge of dysfunction.

In theory USACA's elections for its board of directors were supposed to happen every two years. USACA's constitution divided the country into eight regions, and every club which has paid its USACA membership dues (at that time a mere $30 per year) was allowed to elect a director for their region. Due to its size New York had two regional directors, and the member leagues of the USACA elect their own representative. These ten directors elect the USACA executive every two years, with the executive's terms overlapping those of the board.

But the deadline for elections in July 2004 came and went and nothing happened. Then problems arose over a procedure called a background check, which as the name suggests was to make sure that all nominees were of a sound moral character. It was not certain in the USACA who should conduct these checks. Eventually president Gladstone Dainty delegated treasuer Selwych Caesar to this task.

Should a treasurer be doing this? At this point USACA secretary Bobby Refaie raised objections about the membership lists Caesar was using. Caesar insisted on his rights as treasurer to review and certify the membership lists. But Refaie pointed out it was his constitutional right to communicate with the independent auditor on what membership lists he was using to conduct the elections. Eventually an official membership list was published, but it contained some strange omissions and errors, which went unexplained by Caesar.

Refaie received a list of nominees from the independent auditor and made this list available to other USACA officers. He then proceeded to streamline the list, losing the names of those who had decided not to run after all, and published this on the USACA website.

Following this Caesar published his own final list of nominees, based on his background check. It retained the names dropped by Refaie – it appears that Caesar had not been informed that some of the nominees had dropped out. And crucially Caesar excluded several nominees who had not submitted their forms or paid their background check fees on time.

There was a brutal logic behind all this conniving. The Caesar list would include several elections that would be uncontested and would hand the election to the incumbent Dainty regime. At this point Refaie instructed the independent auditor to cease all activities with the USACA elections indefinitely.

From the outside all this political manoeuvring looked ridiculous, like ants fighting over a crumb of food. But it did not go unnoticed. The ICC sent a letter to Gladstone Dainty voicing its displeasure over the infighting and warning him that if USACA did not sign a document called a Memorandum of Understanding over Project USA that if would cancel the whole initiative. 'We have seen numerous sporting organisations in various states of disarray throughout our period of involvement as sports administrators,' it said witheringly. 'We have never seen a sporting organisation that combines such great potential and such poor administration as USACA. From our observations, much of the blame for this lies with the current office bearers of USACA, including yourself. We question whether the current administration of USACA can play any constructive role in taking the game forward in the United States.'

But the warning went unheeded. Dainty did not sign the Memorandum and Project USA was cancelled.

This in turn prompted a rebellion within the organisation. A group called the Council of League Presidents (CLP) emerged calling for reform of US cricket's system of governance. USACA sued the seven members of its interim council. The CLP sued back and then … nothing seemed to happen. A compromise would eventually be worked out, but Project USA was irretrievable.

In the meantime the ICC decided to suspend USACA in August 2005 with then-ICC chief executive Malcolm Speed admonishing all concerned: 'Neither party should see this outcome as a victory. Regrettably, the game of cricket in the USA and the cricketers who seek to play cricket for USA at the highest level are again the losers.'

It was during this time that we caught up with USACA president Gladstone Dainty, the spider at the centre of this web of intrigue. We met at the Hilton Hotel in Washington

DC, the city where he has lived since he moved to the US from Guyana in the early 1970s and where he still practised as a chartered accountant.

He was exactly how we pictured him, a rotund Caribbean gentleman in his 50s. We ordered coffees, while Dainty helped himself to a muffin which he proceeded to scoff, talking whilst his mouth was full. Small pieces of muffin flew out on to the table when he made a point.

Regarding the failure of Project USA, he gave his reasons why he rejected it. It was the lack of control and by implication – though he didn't use the phrase during our conversation – the ICC's patronising 'colonialist' outlook.

'From my standpoint you get this feeling that they seem to have the idea that because you are an associate member you are also an associate person. For me what was very revealing was that, while I was in England recently, Malcolm Speed actually looked at me straight in the face and told me to shut up when I was expressing an opinion. He told me to shut up. I don't know what gives people the right to be that condescending.

'I was never against Project USA,' he maintained. 'I was always for it. What I was against was the idea that monies raised in America … their first suggestion was to take that money to Monaco, and then they [the ICC] would release it in blocks of $100,000.'

This fed in to this other objection, that it threatened USACA's charitable status. 'We're a 50123 corporation or entity in the US. We enjoy tax holidays, so if you have this money as a 50123 the key element is control. So once Malcolm Speed can collect and control the money that, you know, once … but [as a 50123 entity] in order for you to remain legal, the control must lie in the US.'

The ICC was suggesting, he argued, that USACA wasn't grown-up enough to control the money. 'The implication and suggestion was that maybe people are squandering the money. In this country, that is illegal. You can go to jail for something like that. If you do that you have to be careful because what if you succeed and I lose everything because of a false accusation?'

He wouldn't comment on the criticisms of the CLP, since at that point it was still a live action. But when we asked him about USACA's reputation for amateurish bungling he brushed it off. 'One of the prerequisites for control among the cricketing community seem to be silence or a lack of complaints to the ICC. Americans are a different race. People will complain. There will always be a strong opposition. And in my opinion sometimes people overreact, to complain.

'There has been this talk in the US about this administration, none of us are quote-unquote "good enough",' he said, naming the names of his supporters on the board. 'Maybe you have to look some kind of way, act a certain kind of way for you to be "good enough". Maybe. I'm not accusing anyone of anything else. What I'm saying is that all of those people, you know …. it's just constant attacks. Among those people [who supported him] you have a businessman, a diplomat, a banker, a successful businessman. You've got achievers among those people but suddenly when it comes to cricket they are deadbeats. They're losers.

'Allowing an administration to raise and administer the sport is important. It's a whole lot better. Running a few games and hoping they bring in a few dollars is not going to work. There is no history of any international organisation really successfully bringing one of these countries into the professional mode. It happens from within. The traditionally strong cricketing nations – Australia, England, West Indies, New Zealand, India, South Africa and Pakistan – were not creations of a quote-unquote ICC "marketing operation". They came from the bottom up. So I think the ICC's role should be to enhance what are the special circumstances that's going on here. Just throwing a bunch of money is not necessarily going to work. Money is important but we've got to bring it up from the grassroots.'

At times he sounded pugnacious, saying: 'I'm American, I'm not going to let someone come from outside the country and stick it to me unnecessarily. In addition to what I said, I'm not going to go looking for fights. But if you start a fight I'm not going to run away from it. I'm not running from this. Whether I'm president or prime minister or whatever, I'm going to do my piece. I'm going to stick around.'

At other times, though, he sounded sad, almost wistful, describing cricket administrators as 'addicts'. 'The structure of cricket in the United States, the way it is set up, the foundation, is addiction. And because the foundation is addiction we're not going to throw them aside, cast them aside just like any other junkie.

'For a lot of people they think that cricket needs us. For me, it's different. I need cricket. That's end of story. Cricket don't need me. I need cricket.'

By way of an illustration, he told us a story of how obsessed he was by cricket as a little boy in Guyana. 'I lived on the west of Guyana. They had cricket in the village on Sundays. So as a little kid you go and help roll the pitch or whatever where the big guys are playing. Sunday was for homework and my mother said "there's no cricket". I said "OK". So she told me to take my clothes off. I mean I was maybe about eight years old so it was all my clothes. Stripped naked. She didn't trust me. She thought I'd go out and watch cricket. So she said she wouldn't trust me. We had an outhouse, you know. I said, "Mummy I want to go out to the garden." She told me, "You can't go out naked, you haven't got any clothes on."

'Then she said, "Tell you what, put one of my blouses on, run real fast and come back." Needless to say she didn't see me until that evening. I was out of there, just the blouse on, no shorts, no nothing, sitting in a tree looking at my cricket. How in the world are you going to get rid of a guy like this? I love this thing. I live this thing – understand what I mean. And what I love is cricket.'

And so the enduring image Gladstone Dainty leaves us with that day is of the most powerful man in American cricket perched in a tree, dressed in nothing but his mother's blouse.

Doubtless Dainty was thinking that by describing himself as a cricketing junkie he was seeking to portray himself in a positive light, as a man of dogged obsession, driven by a deep passion for the sport. But as anyone who has lived with one knows, junkies exhaust the patience of their family and friends. Relationships are destroyed because, in thrall to their addiction and unable to see the bigger picture, the junkie is unaware of the damage they are inflicting on themselves and others.

And so it was with Dainty and the men who ran USACA. Cricket gave shape and meaning to their lives. Unable to play anymore, moving into administration gave them standing within their communities, a sense of self-worth and, as they moved up the ladder, the delicious taste of power. And as even the most selfless of politicians can attest to, giving that up can be very difficult.

* * *

A few months later in Sri Lanka we met the USACA treasurer Selwyn Caesar. A Trinidadian, who at that point was already several years retired, he was candid about the financial difficulties cricket faces in America.

He explained that the annual stipend from the ICC at that time was just $54,000. USACA received funding from ICC Americas for their under-19 and under-15 teams and for any national youth programme. And that's it. It hardly touched the sides.

'Funding from the private sector is at this point extremely difficult,' he said. 'We have had several enquiries from firms. What usually happens, we do receive donations from individuals. For instance, our vendor who provides the colour clothing – Mr Singh, and the vendor who provides most of the airline travel, Mr Bowler. Sometimes he gives us a few free tickets and extra donations.'

And corporate sponsorship? 'It's not for the lack of trying,' he shrugged. 'We appointed several people who were classified as marketing or financial people to source corporate sponsorship but generally the first question that is asked is "what is cricket?"

'One time I tried to explain to one of the people from the ICC that if we have an executive board meeting comprised of five people it would cost us close to $45,000. The cost of travel, hotel, meeting rooms etc. [We were speaking in the days before Skype and Zoom.] And he could not comprehend that. California and New York are three and a half, four hours apart. I've just finished my budget for 2006 and meetings alone is close to $50,000.'

Private investors need to first see a 'product'. 'I would say without fair contradiction, without creating any friction, that we haven't got the product,' Caesar admitted. There was no national league, no pyramid structure that could possibly entice investors. US cricket, he explained, was caught in a chicken and egg situation. There couldn't be a product without investment, but no investment could ever come without the product.

The lack of a pyramid also had an effect on the national team. All too often selection policy wasn't based on player meritocracy, but on placating the egos of regional directors. 'If you are a regional director in California you've got five guys who should come to trials for the national team,' he said. 'But under the scheme of things those five guys can't even make a second division team under the normal process. And if you are from Chicago you've also got five guys. There's no concept that you are looking for the best players in the country. The concept is that you try to satisfy the directors.'

Caesar also talked of the way individuals like himself have had to dip into their own pockets to ensure players are able to make it to tournaments. The ICC only funded national teams to arrive from a certain point, in the US usually New York or New Jersey. But of course, the players from California, Texas and Florida all had to travel long distances just to arrive at that departure point, journeys which the ICC do not fund. 'Public criticism is not an easy thing. They talk about misappropriation of funds – I paid the travel agent $200,000 and I paid the vendor for cricket equipment $100,000. That's $300,000.

'My phone bill every month is over $500. I mean my wife asked me the other day why I'm always still up at two o'clock in the morning. I'm having to phone Dubai [where the ICC's headquarters are].'

In the end we felt sorry for Caesar. He seemed tired of all the politics, the constant criticism and carping and was ready for an easier life in retirement. But speaking to him did throw light on the specific problems a national body like USACA faced – the geographical and logistical challenges, the financial ones, but most of all the sheer amount of workload involved. Organising the governance of a sport in a country the size of the US was an immense task, and yet it was being done by part-timers, and in Caesar's case, a retiree.

Meanwhile, by 2005 there was another rival to USACA rising – Bernard Cameron's Major League Cricket (see chapter 6). Cameron had written to the ICC requesting that they recognise his organisation as the governing body in the US. But the ICC, perhaps preferring to deal with the devil they knew and tiring of the whole circus, chose this moment – March 2006 – to lift USACA's suspension. On certain criteria.

Those were the elections for the board had to be completed by December that year and that these should be overseen by a third party and under 'an agreed constitution', meaning one that had been approved by the ICC. The world governing body added that the 'ICC executive board reserves the right to revert to the previous position of withholding funds and not recognising the USACA at ICC events/meetings, etc., if any of the above conditions are not met.' In other words, USACA were on probation.

A draft constitution had been put together by September that year, but new elections still had not taken place three months later. When these finally happened the following February they were conducted with undue haste, with many complaining that they had little time to organise. The ICC extended the deadline to the start of March 2007, but when that passed, they were suspended once more.

Throughout most of 2007 consultations and negotiations took place between Dainty and his followers and the rebels from the Council of League Presidents. One of these sit-downs took place in Washington in June with the West Indies board president Ken Gordon acting as peacemaker. Eventually an agreement was reached to appoint a 'reconciliation commission' headed by John Aaron, which would examine the new constitution and try to find a way forward that would be agreeable to all parties.

The following January we met John Aaron near his home in Queens. A genial fellow who looked a decade younger than the 58 he was, he was another Guyanese American who came from a cricketing family – his father was a commentator and writer whilst his brother played to a fairly high standard in Guyana. An administrator for his club Atlantis, he too seemed to be motivated by the vague idea of 'giving something back', though he seemed less motivated by personal glory. If he was a cricket junkie then, unlike Dainty, Aaron's habit was well under control.

'I was encouraged by people who said, "You know you can make a difference,"' he smiles. 'After we had the second suspension I said, "This is it you know, if I am going to get in ..." My wife said, "You've got one leg in and one leg out!

You either jump right in and go and do what you've got to do or don't do anything." I said, "You're right." So I jumped in and we formed the Reconciliation Commission.

'The mission statement of the Commission was to get USACA as it was then to come to the table and say, "Let's resolve the issues that are causing problems with cricket." We approached them, we sent them a letter. Didn't respond. Sent a letter to the president. Still didn't respond. So we got into a bit of a telephone tiff and I said, "Look, you've got to respect this group because this group represents the league presidents." He [Dainty] obviously perceived this as a threat.'

Aaron, though, had honest intentions. 'He misunderstood our mission, which was not to seek office but to finally resolve the issue. I'm saying to myself, "This makes no sense for us to sit here and twiddle our thumbs and wait for this guy. Why don't we try to resolve our differences now? Let's try and hammer out the differences, come up with a framework with you as the chairperson, agree to it and this is the framework for going forward." He thought that's a great idea and he summoned a meeting in Washington DC.'

Eventually these negotiations led to a new constitution which was approved by USACA's membership in January 2008. The turnout though was low – only 180 of the 677 eligible clubs voted in the end. This meant that a couple of months later, fresh elections could at long last be held. However, any idea that the slate might be wiped clean and US cricket might greet a bright new dawn was swiftly curtailed – Gladstone Dainty was re-elected by a thin majority of three votes. The ICC re-admitted USACA.

There were some stipulations though, one of which was that USACA had to appoint a chief executive, a person who – in theory – would be the figurehead of cricket in the United States, someone who would be able to make the deals that could finally unlock the treasure trove that everyone assumed lay at the end of the rainbow. 'Obviously he takes his orders from the board,' explained Aaron, who had by now been elevated to USACA secretary. 'But the board has the vision. He implements that vision. So he must be in concert with that vision. But clearly he will run the day-to-day operations in terms of negotiating contracts, fundraising activities, management of an office.'

In March 2009, USACA got their man: a sports administrator and event organiser named Don Lockerbie. Lockerbie certainly had an impressive CV – a white American with an more than decent track record, he had been a senior consultant for the 1994 FIFA World Cup in the States – he'd been in charge of the planning and construction at Giants Stadium in New Jersey, where he had to make sure the venue had a turf pitch that was up to scratch. He'd also done venue planning at the Atlanta Olympics. More relevant to USACA, Lockerbie had also been chief operating officer in the recent cricket World Cup in the West Indies. He seemed to tick all the boxes.

He talked a good fight too. Early on, Lockerbie spoke about 'Project 15', a target he had to get the USA into the world's top 15 nations with an eye to qualification for the 2015 World Cup. He talked not only of recruiting a top coach for the national team, but a common coaching philosophy that would develop world class teams at all levels, as well as central playing contracts, healthcare benefits and educational opportunities for players. Then there was his idea of 'Destination USA', of promoting the USA as a neutral venue for international friendlies. This would, of course, involve the building of new stadiums – but wasn't that what Lockerbie was good at anyway? America's cricket fraternity had good reason to be optimistic.

And by the end of the year, Lockerbie – to his credit – had pulled off a coup. In November 2009, it was announced that the USA would enter into a 'strategic partnership' with New Zealand cricket. This mainly appeared to involve the sharing of coaching and developmental resources, as well as a promise to stage some New Zealand internationals in the States. And indeed six months later this latter promise was fulfilled when the Black Caps took on Sri Lanka in a three-match T20 series staged at Broward County in Florida. It was the first time two full ICC members had played together on American soil.

However, somewhat embarrassingly, the first game – a night-time fixture – was cancelled when it was declared the stadium's floodlights were unfit to host international cricket. Of course, it could have easily been played earlier in the day, but Lockerbie maintained that the cancellation was nothing to do with poor ticket sales. Oh no. 'We feel it's better to start with a big bang on the weekend,' he told *Cricinfo*.

In the end, though, there were grumblings about the slow pitch, fans did show up at the two remaining games and the series was drawn 1-1. But it seemed, if nothing else, like a start.

In fact, it was the end. 'That was a real shenanigans that was,' remembers Imran Khan, the then-US manager. 'The New Zealanders were adamant that there was nothing going on after that. The pitch was awful, the facilities were club class, and I don't think they were very impressed with the way it was organised. Plus I don't think they generated the revenue that they wanted to – they lost a lot of money.'

By November 2010, Lockerbie himself had gone; ousted, it seems, in another USACA power struggle. Neither side provided an explanation at the time, and it was left to others to guess what had gone on behind the scenes.

Khan, who had spent extended periods of time with him as part of the national team set-up, had been less than impressed. 'He promised a lot. He travelled round the country, he spoke to all the cricket boards, he tried to get people on board. It really seemed like he was doing a lot. You saw that with all the photo ops he did. Anywhere he could give a speech, he gave a speech. He was promising these wild, almost ludicrous deals that he was going to offer players.

'He constructed a lot of the stadiums – there was one in Antigua which had to be abandoned while England were playing a Test match but a lot of people have referred to him as a bullshitter. He also claimed that he was working on the Olympic Stadium in London. To my knowledge he had no part to play in that stadium. He said he was building a stadium in Indianapolis – the council hadn't even decided or deliberated on it or talked about or heard about such a proposal. There were other projects that he talked about that never happened.'

It took 11 years for Lockerbie to give his version of events on Peter Della Penna's *Stars and Stripes* podcast.

It seems that it was when the USACA board was on the verge of actually dotting the i's and crossing the t's on the

New Zealand deal, they had their heads turned by some other investors who were proposing to set up a T20 league in the US. 'I insulted the board and when you do that, you get terminated. But I was serious. I could see that the New Zealand deal was going to fail because of some hidden agendas I wasn't aware of, and I was just angry.

'I brought a deal to the table that would change USA cricket forever, with one of the great federations. The US constitution was still a mess and Cricket New Zealand were going to help us restructure. We were going to do the whole thing – a new constitution, new election by-laws, redo the whole narrative and I think that's what they were upset about. I think they feared for their positions.'

Nevertheless, the New Zealand deal went ahead. The partnership formed a new entity called Cricket Holdings America which held the rights to a potential T20 franchise league. As part of the deal, New Zealand agreed to play a number of matches in the US and to make its players available for that T20 league. None of this would ever come to pass.

Meanwhile, with Lockerbie gone there were no barriers to Dainty consolidating his power further. Increasingly thin-skinned, he seemed determined to alienate even those board members who were trying to seek a middle way, like John Aaron. The secretary was suspended, and

Dainty took extreme action to stop him attending board meetings.

Ostensibly, this was over a piece the secretary had written on the website usacricketers.com about a meeting of the New York board that Dainty had unexpectedly attended, and which had then deteriorated into an argument about finances. 'I penned the piece saying that Dainty showed up and used the phrase "a presidential visit that was anything but presidential" because he started cursing. So based on me writing that piece on a website he suspended me from the board. I got a letter saying "John, you're suspended until the next board meeting convenes and the board decides otherwise."

'It was six months before he scheduled a board meeting. When I got to the board meeting – we're staying in the same hotel and in the lobby it didn't say "USACA meeting", it said "Gladstone Dainty meeting" – he booked the meeting under his name so he could control who comes into the meeting, right? Which is fine. So myself and three other guys walked up to the meeting and when we turned the corner there was this uniformed police officer."

'They had a list and I was thinking, "Uh oh, I'm sure my name isn't on that list." But I was wearing a USACA jacket with a blazer with the logo. I had my laptop, I had files so I guess to the officers I looked like I belonged in there. So I walked in and sat down.

'Dainty comes in and Dainty is sitting here and I'm sitting there, and Dainty is like, "You know you're not supposed to be in this meeting here, right?" "Really? Why?" He said, "Because you're suspended." I said, "By who?" "I suspended you." "But you don't have the right to – only the board can decide to." "Well, you're not supposed to be here." "I'm here doing my job," and he got up and he went outside. He went outside to the cop. The cop come in and asked me to step outside. I said, "No problem," and I got up.

'The cop said, "I don't understand this guy!", meaning Dainty. Because he had hired the cop – the expense that he went to. The cop says, "I never heard about this at a cricket meeting!" He said, "When some of the soccer guys come into town they hire us to keep their ladies from banging on the guys' doors and getting in there, but not for a cricket meeting!"'

* * *

By this time fresh USACA board elections were supposed to have taken place but had been postponed. Then when they did happen the following year, they were subject to gerrymandering on such a scale it was laughable.

Of the 47 leagues that could vote in the board elections, Dainty had ruled that 32 of them were 'non-compliant'. The way he managed to do this was via an audit conducted by an attorney with the somewhat apt name of Robert Chance. Chance had come up with nine criteria by which a league could be deemed to be 'complaint', which included some such things as whether the league had a women's or youth section. None of the 47 leagues had all nine, but the way the information was applied appeared to be inconsistent. For example, the Midwest Cricket Conference met eight out of the nine criteria, as did the Great Lakes Cricket Conference. However, while the latter were approved as compliant, the former were not.

Talking to *Cricinfo*, Michael Gale, USACA's vice president at the time, attempted to explain this away, by saying: 'You're assuming that all the nine variables are equal. For example, few if any leagues had either a youth or a women's development plan in place ... it's not the number of variables that were covered, but the magnitude of those variables which were really important.' He then refused to comment on individual leagues' cases.

It was, of course, all a ruse to stop Dainty's critics from voting him out. 'This is a big farce,' USACA board member Krish Prasad told *Cricinfo* at the time. 'This is the total destruction for United States cricket and an embarrassment.'

'[Dainty] didn't want Eastern American [an anti-Dainty league] on that list because Eastern American has been challenging him for [what] he's been doing and he knows that's not a vote for him,' Prasad said. 'So, if it's not a vote for him, then why put them on the list? He puts just about every league that would support him and vote for him.'

And lo and behold when the elections were held in March 2010 the incumbent won by a landslide, by 12 votes to two. Dainty and his cabal had long used underhand methods to retain control, but never before in such a blatantly dishonest manner. For many, it was the final straw.

Within weeks 20 of the leagues that had been shut out of the election met to discuss a way forward. In May they announced that they were forming a new breakaway organisation, Cricket America, which was quickly renamed the American Cricket Federation (ACF). 'The need for transparency, authentic political inclusion and effective participation of all members in the decision-making process are the founding principles of Cricket America. We believe that the way forward for cricket in the USA is inclusion and not exclusion,' said Leighton Greenidge, president of Southern Connecticut Cricket Association, who was on the new body's steering committee.

The idea was to create a body that was the mirror image of USACA, one that was open to all, democratic, transparent and encouraged and welcomed women's and youth cricket. The aim was to grow and eventually convince the ICC that it should be the national governing body, rather than USACA. The end game was approaching.

The ACF moved fast. By the October of that year it had organised its first national tournament, the first of any kind in the US for 15 months, and it had received a major boost when the Southern California Cricket Association – the largest league on the west coast – gave its support.

Meanwhile, by the following spring USACA had appointed a new CEO. Darren Beazley was an Aussie who had had some success in South Africa growing the sport of Aussie Rules football, as well as being the CEO of Perth's 2011 World Sailing Championships. Unlike Lockerbie, he seemed aware of the scale of his task, telling *Cricinfo*: 'There'll be a lot of Doubting Thomases and a lot of people telling, "USACA, you can't do it," and giving us a million reasons why not. I'm not saying that everything I've got in my mind will come to fruition, but I can tell you now we're certainly going to give it our best shot.

'I'm not going to ride in on a white horse and wave a magic wand and all of the issues are going to go away because that's not how sport works anywhere in the world, but I am coming here saying that I'm here to help. I'm here to work with people and if we do that together then my experience has been over such a long period of time that success becomes inevitable.'

Not everyone was impressed. 'A lot of people were impressed with him and would go "Oh, he's very business savvy, he presents himself in a very professional manner,"' says *Cricinfo*'s Peter Della Penna. 'He knew how to shake hands, pick up a phone and write emails. Those are the USACA qualifications for "professionalism". If you can do those then they think you are a type of hero.

'So he came in and he was a very good meddler. He got involved with things that he had little knowledge of and he tried to stick his fingers in areas where he really should not have. I think he probably felt "Hey, I'm a paid professional, I came from Australia where we have a proper cricket structure. I know how things are supposed to be done. I'm just going to insert myself into the process and show these guys how it's meant to be done."'

One of these was criticising the players. 'He came in and he made all these speeches about "I'm a professional, I'm going to be making the US a professional cricket country and the first step is the players." Instead of saying "I'm going to put professional facilities in place, put professional turf wickets, get professional infrastructure." Once you've got that established then you can focus on putting players on central contracts, whatever. But he said, "No, the players, that's what I'm going to be concentrating on." And I'm going to make them be professional without actually paying them as professionals. So he was sitting in these selection meetings and he was kind of trying to influence things, and meddling in that without having any respect for the players who contributed.'

It seems that Beazley also had his sights set on reforming the administration. USACA had commissioned a report into its governance by TSL Consulting back in 2012 and Beazley, alongside ICC global development manager Tim Anderson, had tried to drum up support for its (mostly sensible) recommendations. These included reducing the size of the USACA board, establishing term limits for board members and introducing player representation on to the board. At the USACA AGM in November 2013 it had been decided to postpone any decision on implementing these. But by the following March, Beazley himself had resigned. He'd lasted just over a year.

At the same time, the ACF were growing in strength. In February New York's largest league – the Commonwealth Cricket League – threw in their lot with the insurgents. Others, including the Mid Atlantic Cricket Conference, Pittsburgh Cricket Association and Florida Southeast Cricket League had followed them too. Struggling for money and with thousands now going out in legal costs, USACA had doubled their annual membership dues from $4,000 to $8,000 and many leagues were voting with their wallets. By now they had less hard-ball leagues than the ACF.

The ICC were watching and in June 2014 they put USACA "on notice" – they were by now clearly not the sole governing body in the country – and gave them a year to sort things out. Unsurprisingly, this did not happen. When the time for the USACA board elections rolled around the following spring, the result was the usual farce. Dainty was re-elected for a third time, with 38 leagues voting. However, many of these seemed to stretch the definition of what a "league" actually is. In an ICC report, it was alleged that 11 of these leagues were "paper" leagues, registered solely for the purpose of supplying Dainty with an extra vote.

This may well have been the final straw and in June 2015 the ICC suspended the USA's membership for the third time in a decade.

It wasn't just the gerrymandering, or the fact that they were clearly no longer the sole governing body in the US, or the lack of a CEO (associate nations were stipulated that they must have). There was also the matter of a $200,000 loan that the ICC had provided to USACA during Darren Beazley's tenure. It had not only not been paid back, but there were doubts any of the money had ever been used for its intended purposes: cricket. Instead it had, in all probability, been used to cover USACA's ballooning legal bill.

By then USACA's debt had risen to $4 million. 'You know how many tournaments that could run, how much cricket that can raise?' said a flabbergasted John Aaron when we met him in 2018. 'So they were digging a hole, digging a hole to get more money and they couldn't find it.

'The law firm that they have hired – McGuire Group – they were charging $795 an hour on increments of 15 minutes. As soon as you pick up the phone – ker-ching, ker-ching, ker-ching. There's a stopwatch going. How do you dig yourself out a hole of that size?'

Even then the ICC – at least on face value – gave USACA an opportunity to sort themselves out. In July 2015 they laid out 39 conditions that it had to meet to be reinstated as an ICC member. These included not only a new constitution and fresh elections, but also stringent financial demands – USACA had to provide all its bank account statements, receipts and invoices since 2013 and federal income tax returns since 2011, as well as a five-year business plan to dig itself out of the mountain of debt. It also demanded evidence that would rebut the allegations that the 11 'paper' leagues were anything more than a vote-catching wheeze.

The world governing body had by this point realised that it would have to get its hands dirty and intervene to clear up this mess. So chief executive David Richardson and head of global development Tim Anderson held a series of town hall meetings as well as pow-wows with both USACA and ACF.

John Aaron had by this point thrown in his lot with the ACF. 'I think the ICC looked at all of that and said, "You know what? Enough is enough. We got to do something here." They had meetings with USACA one day and with ACF the next day.

'Dave Richardson and the whole hierarchy of ICC went in there and there were three of us representing the board and we laid out what our intention was. Our intention was to become the national governing body. But we realised we couldn't do that without the approval of the ICC and the ICC's hands were somewhat tied because USACA could easily say, "Hey, I was here before and I have a legitimate claim." They would have a battle on their hands.'

The ICC set up four national advisory groups that would implement a strategy for taking the game forward in the US, which would include administrators and players, and significantly female players for the first time (USACA had yet to be graced by the presence of any woman on its board). One of these would draw up a new constitution. When the June deadline passed, the ICC extended it to December, giving the old governing body every chance to do the right thing.

USACA decided that if it was to go down then it would go down fighting and sent a three-page letter to the ICC, vowing that it would 'take action' against the governing body's ultimatum. The letter warned that they had brought in former secretary Kenwyn Williams (who had been suspended as secretary over a social media meltdown in 2012) to help the board in a legal capacity: 'Mr Williams will be tasked with rebuilding our credibility, restoring our public image and economic sustainability in anticipation of the ICC's sustained suspension with constant threats to remove us in December 2016. Mr Williams has experience in the areas of sport litigation and will be responsible for advocating and protecting all the rights of USACA.' Then to prove they meant business they fired off a lawsuit in an attempt to stop some Caribbean Premier League matches being played at the Broward County stadium in Lauderhill (they claimed that the CPL had bypassed them as the governing body). The games went ahead as planned.

By December 2016 work on a new constitution had been completed and the ICC appeared satisfied with the results. These included term limits for all positions, three independent directors and two player directors – one male and one female. They extended the deadline for USACA to ratify this new outline to 1 April 2017.

April Fools' Day came and went. Eventually USACA announced that they had voted against ratifying the new ICC-approved constitution. Amongst their objections were the idea of the body having an independent chairman for the first three years, a figure that had had no previous administrative role in cricket, and the call for fresh elections in the October. USACA wanted them in February 2018 as usual – Dainty clearly wanted to continue his three-year term as president.

The ICC tabled a motion expelling USACA at the annual conference in June. Knowing that their ship was sinking, USACA put out a statement describing the decision as 'manifestly unfair, prejudicial, unlawful, and unreasonable', complaining that: 'The ICC does not want a strong and unified, democratically governed, US cricket community. It wants one that the ICC will control and dominate,' and threatened legal action. In June 2017, after 52 years as a member of the ICC, the USA were finally expelled.

For most of those who had played and lived US cricket, there was no joy. Just relief, tempered with a little sadness. 'I think USACA kept us back 15 to 20 years,' reflected John Aaron the following year. 'I mean at some point in time Dainty must have meant well, but I think as he got more and more involved he realised it was an opportunity for himself and so he started focusing on that.'

The addict had been finally cut off from his supply. This time the sunlight was peeking through the curtains; a new dawn really had arrived. US cricket would be able to start again and finally fulfil its potential. Wouldn't it?

5

The Long and Winding Road

The travails of the men's national team

THE APPEARANCE in the Champions Trophy in 2004 had been an opportunity to show that the US had a cricket team that truly were one of the best 12 in the world. But as we saw at the beginning of our odyssey it was a test they well and truly flunked. The Australia game was pitiful – as you would expect, the best cricket team in the world at the time showed absolutely no mercy to the US part-timers. But their other game, played three days before, at the Oval, was almost as bad.

After a delayed start due to heavy rain, New Zealand scored a whopping 347, with Nathan Astle contributing 145 of those and Craig McMillan 64. The Black Caps had started slowly and at 43/2 you might have been forgiven for thinking an upset could possibly be on the cards. But once McMillan joined Astle in the 43rd over, the pair pummelled the tired US bowlers, scoring 136 in the last eight overs alone.

The US had no reply to that and struggled to 137 all out. New Zealand's 210-run win was up to that point the largest margin of victory in terms of runs in ODIs. Three days later came the humiliation at the Rose Bowl. It would be another 20 years before the US national team would compete again against the Test-playing nations in an ICC competition.

What happened in between was a long and fitful journey full of false dawns, fresh starts and some depressing nadirs. We followed the team – and the under-19 squad – to a number of these competitions around the world, where the associate nations play away from the glare of the spotlight. The attendances were often pitiful, with scorers and media often outnumbering spectators; international sport at its most unglamorous.

And yet, despite the games in the ICC Trophy, the US national team had reason to be optimistic at the end of 2004. After all, they had qualified for that competition by winning the Six Nations Challenge earlier on in the year in Dubai. There they had topped an incredibly tight group that included the Netherlands, Scotland and Canada – all of whom had recently played in the 2003 World Cup. Okay, they had done it only on a superior run rate, but they had beaten Scotland – one of the traditionally strong associate nations.

So going into the ICC Trophy the following year in Ireland they had reasonable grounds for hope. This was the qualifying tournament for the next World Cup in 2007 and drawn in a group with the hosts, Denmark, Uganda, the UAE (whom they'd beaten the previous year in Dubai), Uganda and tiny Bermuda, the US were expected to make the semis, at least.

Instead it was a disaster. The US started badly, losing to the UAE, and then got worse. The following day they were clobbered by Denmark, losing by 96 runs. The following day came the crunch game. Uganda also had yet to register a win. Finally, the US started scoring some runs and managed to get over the 200 mark for the first time – Steve Massiah, the right-hand bat who had once played for Guyana's under-19s, scored an elegant 108. But the Ugandans batted proficiently and aside from Massiah again – who grabbed two wickets – none of the US bowlers could make much of an impact. Uganda overtook the US total with a couple of overs and six wickets to spare.

Afterwards the US team were very despondent. 'We're struggling right now but I think we will come back strong, as we always do,' said Aijaz Ali, the Pakistan-born all-rounder for whom the ICC Trophy would be their final tournament.

'I think we are just adjusting to the weather and the system and the wickets. We only play weekend cricket. It's very tough to come here and compete in a competition like this. We are down but not out. We had a big talk and I think we will come back strong.'

'The spirit is kind of down,' said Clayton Lambert, himself an ex-West Indies Test player. 'You know it's like there is a whole lot of stuff that has been going on and yes, I would say along the way some of the guys are … we felt that "hey this thing was not going to trouble us" but it certainly has. We started preparing a bit late and this is the end result now. We are three games down. We have to try and fight back.'

That 'whole lot of stuff' was the wrangling behind the scenes at USACA (as detailed in chapter 4). When we spoke to Masood Chic, one of the Dainty loyalists who was in Ireland in an official capacity which seemed unclear to us, even he admitted that it had been damaging: 'First of all it has an effect on players. These players, the other opposition group [the Council of League Presidents] was talking about selecting a team also. And these players were confused where to go. Because the players don't know, they are confused whose group is in control. We don't have a practice session.

'When we were preparing for Sharjah [the previous year] there was a different attitude amongst the players. They were very happy. This is so different. We have meetings and they are very serious meetings. We don't joke around. Before it was all fun and things were happening. The spirit is lost.'

It was something of a blessing then that the following day's game against Ireland was a washout, saving the team from further humiliation. It was a brief respite. Instead the US (population 300 million) completed a truly miserable week by losing to Bermuda (population 60,000) in their final group game. And 'losing' doesn't really do justice to what happened. USA won the toss and as usual put Bermuda in to bat. They posted a brilliant 318/8 with Janeiro Tucker scoring 132. Yet again the US couldn't even reach 200. Four of their wickets were taken by a 20-stone spinner named Dwayne 'Sluggy' Leverock.

The US finished bottom of their group and ended up ninth overall. This relegated them to Division One of the new World Cricket League. This was the system that the ICC had set up to provide a pathway for associate nations to qualify for the World Cup and attain ODI status as well as creating a constant stream of meaningful cricket that would – in theory – develop the game.

But before they could even compete in this, the ICC had suspended the US. It meant that when the national team did re-emerge on to the world stage, it would be several divisions lower.

The suspension was supposed to punish the administrators of USACA, so when it came to the under-19 squad, the ICC took pity on the youngsters and allowed them to compete in the Under-19 World Cup, played in Sri Lanka in February 2006, which they had qualified for the previous year, just before the ban came into force.

Here, the youngsters were up against some of the best players in their age group in the world. Drawn in a 'group of death' alongside South Africa, Australia and the West Indies, they stood little chance of getting through to the quarter-finals, though to their credit they gave the West Indies a slight scare in their opening match. And they beat Namibia in their plate match to finish a creditable 12th out of 16 teams.

And yet while the team's performance was far from a disaster, there were complaints from those charged with running the team that would become familiar as years went by. The day after their second game we spoke to the team's trainer, Basil Butcher, a relaxed but focused fellow from New Jersey of Guyanese heritage. He was rueing the opening game against the Windies kids.

'We had the West Indies by their throats and we just couldn't finish the job,' he lamented. 'I know the youngsters from Caribbean heritage, they wanted to show their players "we can play with y'all". We can play with them and they showed that they pretty much could. The only difference between our boys and some of them is that we haven't had the exposure some of them have had. It's not a talent problem or anything. It's just that we haven't had as much exposure as them. We haven't been playing as much.

'I did an interview with a guy from one of the papers round here and I told him about the lack of finances and he was surprised. He said, "How can that be? You are from the big United States, the richest country in the world." I said, "Yes, that's the paradox. We actually left the United States like paupers."'

But even allowing for the lack of finances that was a constant for USACA, Butcher felt the preparation had been lacking. 'In an ideal world, we qualified in August and the team should have been picked some time in September. And from September, all the way on through January, they should have been playing as a team, in camps. I mean, not four-day camps, longer than that because their fitness and all those things have to be up to par.

'I mean yesterday, some of them told me "Coach, I was tired." I mean, I've done as much as is humanly possible to get these guys up to some kind of level of fitness. When we met in Florida in December I told all of them, "All of you guys are fit enough to play cricket at the level we're going to play." I gave all of them an exercise programme, taught them all how to do it. Then I even said, "If you can't remember how to do xyz email me – I can explain."

'And when we got back in January I said to them "Well, great! All of you have been doing your programme I guess, because I didn't receive a single email." I got a lot of "yes coach, yes coach." I said to them, "You can't fool me – who did and who didn't?" And that is where you see the lack of concentration, because if you're not fully fit you start to get tired. Mentally you wander.'

Butcher said he'd write a report, highlighting the need to mirror the challenges of the tournament in the preparation. 'I would have liked for them to have played two games in a row so they can go through that experience. Secondly, I would have wanted us to play against the two best teams we are playing in the warm-up, those games back to back, because that is the experience they would have gone through here.'

He put the blame on a governing body that had little experience of playing international cricket. 'I don't know if they really understood what this undertaking was, what challenges these boys are going to be presented with. Had they really understood, maybe there would have been a little more urgency in how these guys should be prepared for this upcoming venture. And it just shows that despite the lack of preparation that we were still able to compete the way we are, so imagine what we could have done if we had better preparation!'

Then there was the lack of team unity and the great unmentionable in US cricketing circles – the dividing line between players of South Asian descent and those with Caribbean heritage.

'Over and over again in this tour we have had occasions where the Indians would be speaking Hindi. And sometimes in the presence of us West Indians, who don't understand a word that they're saying. And we're representing an English-speaking country. My ideal was that, I think it has happened for the most part, I wanted an Indian to room with a West Indian – every one of them. What you're hoping for is that these guys would sit down in a room and they'd talk cricket and talk about their cultures and the differences. But that hasn't happened for one reason or another.

'But this situation is not unique,' he said, rolling his eyes. 'It happens all the time with US teams travelling. You've got the Indians on one side and the West Indian guys on the other. You know, all the time.'

Yet despite all this, the under-19s had acquitted themselves well on the world stage and there was a feeling that this squad might provide a nucleus of the national team going forward. It was a forlorn hope. A few of the squad did – wicketkeeper Akeem Dodson and left-arm spinner Nisarg Patel would later represent the USA at the T20 World Cup. But the vast majority of that team faded quickly into obscurity. Within a couple of years the captain Hemant Punoo would give up cricket entirely.

The national team should have returned to take part in a Division Three tournament in Darwin in May 2007, but USACA had still not resolved their disputes with the ICC and so after their suspension had been lifted, it was reimposed once more in March. It wasn't until the following year that the national team returned, at Division Five level for a 12-team tournament in Jersey.

Here they were rubbing shoulders with the might of Mozambique, Norway and Germany – countries with no cricketing infrastructure whatsoever. And the US did, at least, dispatch these nations with the minimum of fuss, putting them into the semi-finals.

Which is where they met the hosts. Again, the US won the toss and again they put their opponents in to bat. But Jersey's openers made a 122 first-wicket partnership, with their team reaching 220/5. The US team got off to a tricky start – they reached 32/3, recovered slightly and then collapsed, losing their last six wickets for just 37 runs and being bowled out for 136 with over 11 overs to go.

Jersey, a tax haven with a population of just 97,000, had beaten the USA. And defeat meant the US remained once more in Division Five.

* * *

It was around this time that an expat from the UK was appointed as the national team manager. Imran Khan was a cheery, genial fellow who like his more illustrious namesake had once played for Sussex (albeit the juniors) before injury curtailed his career. He had only emigrated in 2006 and through coaching on the west coast had been brought in to the national set-up. 'I was brought into the fold as the result of a review by the national body,' he told us in 2011. 'They had just competed in Jersey and failed miserably. In terms of an actual national structural programme there was none. I remember that first time going there to Florida. Being involved in that sports side of things you're familiar with basic training, schedule/programme formats for the weekend, etc. I get there for a long weekend and there's nothing. There's no schedule, there's no format, there's no agenda. I was kind of shocked.'

Khan had been brought in for an upcoming series of games in Guyana in November 2008. 'It was a real ad hoc political appointment because we in the west had done really well. And it had always been East Coast dominated – New

York, Florida, etc., so they wanted to make amends.' He would soon become acquainted with the USA's slapdash approach to running a national team.

Together with Clayton Lambert – who was now coach – he tried to initiate a number of reforms. Khan had wanted to create a national database of players so that selectors would have stats at their fingertips. 'The only thing we got was with the national tournament where the regions compete, we got to standardise that a bit more. Whereas before it was just played and the results were faxed in and people sent whatever they wanted. Now we actually had the selectors present.'

Khan brought in a fitness programme, which all selected players were obliged to follow. Players who showed extra ability would get the requisite extra funding, which led to two players – Muhammad Ghous and Adrian Gordon – training with Nottinghamshire CC for a couple of months. 'That was a success, I suppose,' Khan reflects. 'But it was horribly done. I mean the air ticket was covered by USACA, the accommodation was covered by Notts, but they themselves had no stipend. USACA's argument was "At least we paid for them to travel, so therefore we've done our bit, we've sent them to England." Well, you're the national body, you're supposed to do so much more for them!'

Khan, like many others who had come in to the national team set-up with good intentions, found himself stymied by the dysfunction at the heart of USACA. 'It was a difficult relationship I had with the administrators,' he reflects. 'There was an uneasy respect between both camps. A lot of people didn't want me there because they saw me as being politically appointed, which is fine, because I was. But then they also realised that I could do the job, so they just left it at that. It was a very frustrating working relationship because you could clearly see that something needed to be done and no one was doing it.'

Nothing was more frustrating than the selection of players for the national team way past their prime. The US had been laughed at on the international stage at the 2004 Champions Trophy for fielding forty-somethings against the world's best team. But as late as Khan's era (2008–11) it was still going on.

'It's nepotism. A second-string US team of young players went to Bermuda and won the inaugural T20 cup against the same Canada side that went to the World Cup. And we beat them in the final.

'Those guys were discarded like this,' he says as he clicks his fingers. 'Not even a second thought was paid to them and that was what really ticked me off because not only are you destroying the morale of those players, at the end of the day you are effectively making a statement which is saying, "If you're not part of the clique or the group of people we respect and care about, then you've got no chance."

'Then a number of guys continued to play for the US who should never have been there. They've never played in national league tournaments, but haven't really done anything to justify their selection or their time is simply up. I mean they hadn't performed.

'There were a number of selections for the last tournament – which I wasn't part of – down in Florida where they were qualifying for the World Cup, T20s again, but a number of strange selections. (Right-handed batsman and prolific run-scorer Sushil Nadkarni was dropped and then reinstated as the vice-captain.) Then the team went up to Canada and there were a number of players brought in who weren't even named in the squad. Other guys were given an opportunity who were not even being picked for their regional, let alone club, teams. It was clear nepotism, corruption. It's all down to votes and favours.'

Khan alleges that there was interference from the very top: Gladstone Dainty. The president allegedly lobbied to get a particular player into the squad. 'It happened in Guyana, the first tour that we did and I actually had a blow-up with him in Guyana. This happened in the selection before we went to UAE and Nepal, where we actually held out. The captain, the coach and myself, we stayed strong. But the influence was there to get this particular player in.'

Khan won't name the player in question. 'The guy that he wanted in was pretty much from his country and his village and lived very close to him in Washington. He didn't deserve to be in the nets, let alone go on tour with the US team. And he pressed for him hard. I remember around that time the pressure he was putting on everybody! "I'll sack you" and "I'll get rid of you" and all this. But everybody held strong because we knew we were going into a massive tournament, and we couldn't afford to have such a weak player.'

* * *

After the nadir of Jersey, things started to improve a little. The USA made it out of Division Five in February 2010, topping a table that contained the might of Bahrain, Fiji and Singapore. They continued the upward trajectory in August, when they were promoted from Division Four, beating Argentina, Tanzania, Nepal and the hosts Italy. But that progress came to an abrupt halt in January 2011 when they crashed and burned at the Division Three tournament in Hong Kong.

They had got off to a bad start. Even before they'd left the US there was an incident that players even now talk of as being emblematic of the shambles they had to deal with. Sushil Nadkarni remembers: 'They flew all of us to New York early in the morning and we're all waiting for the head coach to arrive so we can grab lunch and stuff. Then they sent somebody to pick up the coach. An hour or two hours later there's still no coach. They call up the guy who's collecting him and he says, "Hey, I'm waiting at the terminal here and I don't see the coach." So then they call up the coach and he's saying, "I'm waiting at the terminal. I don't see anybody there."'

They were, of course, at different airports. 'Then the USACA guy drives another 30 minutes to the other airport and picks up the coach and checks him into the wrong hotel. Someone had told him that we're all staying in the Holiday Inn next to the airport. The coach had finally arrived at that place at four or five in the evening while we'd been waiting there since morning. Incompetence at its very worst. Unbelievable.'

'Those small moments were funny, though small but were representative of the quality of management,' suggests his team-mate, fast bowler Usman Shuja. 'I was working at IBM at the time so I saw a high quality organisation and then you see this ... circus.'

But unlike circuses, the comedy on display was purely unintentional. Sushil Nadkarni can remember the confusion

133

there was amongst the squad when Dipak Patel was brought on board as coach around 2008. 'He and Clayton Lambert were both coaches on tour and there was so much tension between the two as to who's the head coach and who is doing what. I mean it was funny for us as players to watch, but one coach was saying one thing to one player and the other was saying another to other players. Nobody knew who was calling the shots.

'Then you had the managers who were even more hilarious! The managers were always those positions that were given to folks that were needed to be taken care of. So you had people out there who were there for a vacation basically and then had no idea how to be a manager on tour. And players were demanding X, Y and Z and they were surprised that they had to do this stuff. And then we were like, "Oh yeah, this guy is a political guy. Of course, they're not going to do anything!"'

Usman Shuja later went public with his criticisms of the national team set-up. In a 2015 *Cricinfo* article, he wrote about the poor communication – sometimes he would go up to ten months without hearing anything from the national organisation – and a sheer lack of care for the players. Those who were injured on international duty were given no support, either financial or emotional, by the national body.

Today, he is more philosophical about those years. 'I think we had the talent to do well, if the administration had been good. But even then when you represent the US you have a certain image and we looked very amateur. It's okay to say, "We're not good at sport but we still have some standards of management and performance and fitness." At least we should have represented America in a good way in terms of fitness, how we show up. It's okay to not have the skills because it is an emerging sport. But at least have standards in the other things.'

The preparation for these tournaments was barely there, according to Sushil Nadkarni. 'Preparation was pretty much down to the individual. I think our getting together was more at the airport – that's when we first all saw each other. I don't remember extensive preparation, camps and stuff before big tournaments. We may have had one or two here and there, but as a standard practice I know that didn't take place. A few players like Usman and I kept in touch quite a bit and challenged each other on our preparation going into big tournaments. We had our own gym memberships and did our own practices in our respective areas.'

Basic fitness was a problem. 'I always knew how well we'd do in a tournament because of the time of year it was held,' says Nadkarni. 'If the tournament was in the summer, we'd usually do okay. When we won in Italy in

2010 all of us had been playing regularly for months at that point.

'If it was early in the year, then I'd fear the worst. When we went to Hong Kong the following January, well most of us hadn't played cricket for a few months. In places like California you hadn't been playing since late October, New York even earlier. So we were out of condition and just weren't up to speed. And it showed in those games.'

The US actually won the first game against the home nation fairly easily, Steve Massiah scoring 97. The problems came the following day, in the second game against Denmark. Peter Della Penna, then *Cricinfo* US correspondent, remembers the game as being emblematic. 'They had Denmark three or four down pretty early and then they dropped six or seven chances in that game. It was embarrassing. The captain was dropped on 15, 30 and 50-something and he wound up making something like 77 not out. Denmark finished on 193.

'Denmark is easily one of the worst teams I've seen at associate level. They are awful. They are a very methodical, plodding team. But they are a team who, whilst they don't have any difference-makers, will always score in the 180 to 220 range. They'll never threaten to explode. The bowling is very workmanlike. They make the most out of their abilities and are very disciplined and focused and they are always giving 100% effort and that's what keeps them in the game.

'During the innings break, the USA were so relaxed. Everybody was joking around, nobody was taking things seriously. They thought, "These guys are a bunch of nobodies. 180? We'll knock this off." Guys were just chilling. There was a family there from America that had come to see the game, so having seen this rare demonstration of support the US guys get very relaxed. They invite the kid into the team tent that has been set up and they were signing cricket balls for him, taking pictures with him.

'At 72/3 in their innings, the US are cruising. Lennox Cush plays this ego shot that was totally needless. It was in the air for an eternity, and it's finally caught. Carl Wright, because he had been off strike for now 15 balls, sees the off-spinner and he's like, "I need to do something to get these guys." So, he swings across the line and is out lbw.'

Aditya Thyagarajan, a middle-order batter, comes in. He had already sprained his ankle fielding and in normal circumstances would be resting, but he comes in to bat. 'Because of his ankle injury he is putting extra weight on the opposite leg,' remembers Della Penna. 'He gets this full toss from a leg-spinner. Because they'd lost a bunch of wickets instead of swatting it for four runs he actually tries to show it some respect, so instead of playing it normally he is too conservative and in the process he collapses, tries to readjust his weight and he puts too much pressure on the other leg and winds up dislocating his knee. It was very gruesome. I saw his knee buckle through my lens. That was a psychological blow, because he was the guy who usually got them out of trouble.'

It presaged a full-blown collapse. 'The guys who were left batting you could say were the tail but these guys still can bat, and the standard of bowling that they face in US league cricket is much stronger than what they faced from Denmark. Denmark's bowling was so embarrassing.' In the end the US were all out for 163 with over ten overs remaining.

The rest of the tournament was a disaster. In the following game, on a foggy morning at Hong Kong Cricket Club, the US collapsed to 44 all out against Papua New Guinea. With Thyagarajan injured, the US had decided to turn not to one of the two younger reserves in the squad but 46-year-old assistant coach Howard Johnson. A veteran of the debacle against Australia in 2004, Johnson had not played for the US for six years. It seemed to sum up the paucity of vision. Incredibly, he opened the bowling against PNG, who took just six overs to complete their victory.

They managed to beat Oman in the next game, but their fate was sealed in the final match against Italy. The US posted a respectable 222, which Italy overcame with three overs to spare. They were relegated back to Division Four.

Imran Khan had had a bad feeling about the tournament before it started: 'You could feel it for the first time, because so much corruption and nepotism had taken place, and so many people have been hurt in the process of the last year or so, that inherently this team cannot succeed any more. That luck, that rub of the green that always goes our way is not going to go our way. And it didn't. Aditya broke his knee. We had guys busting their fingers and wrists, guys being given out lbw when the ball hit them in the ribs. Ridiculous stuff. You know being bowled out by Denmark for God's sake, a team my club team could have beaten!'

But then as Khan himself admits the preparation for Hong Kong had been appalling even by US standards. 'Everyone else had gone to Sri Lanka and India or somewhere else. Our guys went out to Asia completely dry. And they'd had no cricket for six months. It was snowing in New York. Most of the guys were from the East Coast so there was no cricket.

'Some of the guys had indoor nets but the facilities were horrible. It's like the ball is bouncing past your face. You're playing on low, skiddy Asian wickets, low and slow turning wickets. These guys are completely unprepared, their fitness levels are horrendous. The first day we had them warm up.

You could see guys huffing and puffing! I know there's a period of acclimatisation, but these were guys who were genuinely unfit.'

There was other stuff too. The players were unhappy because a bonus that had been promised to them after the Italy tournament had still not been paid. Then the kit turned up. 'In a way it was hilarious,' remembers Khan. 'There was a spelling mistake on the badge. Nobody's got numbers on their shirts. Not to mention that there were shirts that didn't even have badges, numbers or names. In fact, three guys in our team didn't even have a kit. They were playing in ours, the managers, coaches and physios' kit.

'I know these are small issues. But there are so many little gripes that they all add up and that's the energy I'm talking about, because at the end people get frustrated and tired and it rubs off on the team. The team isn't happy and people aren't happy because of their stipends and some people aren't getting paid on time and people are being asked to take time off work at short notice.'

The Hong Kong tournament was the end of the road for Khan. The US wouldn't play in a 50-over game for another 18 months, when they managed to get promoted from Division Four. In the following tournament in Bermuda in spring 2013, the US won their first three matches against Nepal, Italy and Oman before familiar problems struck and the team once more snatched defeat from the jaws of victory. They crumbled to just 93 all out against Uganda and also came up short against the might of Bermuda in the final game.

By the middle of the decade it was clear that there had been no long-term improvement. The US had hit a plateau of sustained mediocrity. In the T20 format, they would invariably ease past their rivals in the Americas section – Canada, Argentina, the Cayman Islands and the like – before they were defeated by the bigger fish among the associates: Ireland, Scotland and Netherlands in the global qualifiers to the World Cup. In the 50-over game, they had found their level around Division Three to Four. Given the size and resources of the US it was a pitiful state of affairs.

And it seemed like things were going to get worse before they got better. USACA were suspended from the ICC in 2015 and there were intimations that this time the ICC were serious about putting things in order regarding governance of the US game. Several of the players voted with their feet. Both Steve Massiah and Sushil Nadkarni retired at the end of 2014. The following year Usman Shuja followed them.

'I think it was the right time to step out,' says Shuja today. 'I was still playing well and I was the highest wicket-taker in the last tournament. I was still performing, I was very fit, but they were still questioning whether I should play or not. I just didn't want to deal with it. But most importantly I had lost interest at that point. Physically and mentally I was okay, but emotionally I'd lost interest.'

'It was a tough decision. It's always hard to give up something which you love, but it was also not very hard because I had just had a baby and a job so playing part-time and travelling was just becoming too complicated. But I was very disappointed that there was not a single email or phone call from the USA cricket administration. Up till now there has not been one single recognition of not only representing but also retiring as the leading wicket-taker or anything. That was disappointing.'

For both players there was frustration at what could have been. 'Over the years we had the talent,' reflects Nadkarni. 'Literally, we had many first-class players. I would say many of us really tried to play for our respective countries but didn't make it for one reason or another. So we were not national material for countries, but we were not bad either. We were just … there. We had the talent.

'But the main source of frustration was again and again us players put in a lot of hard work coming into the tournament and we saw it all falling apart because of the lack of organisation on the behalf of the administration. You do the best you can and you really want to make an effort and make it work. A few individuals can't do anything if the entire unit isn't moving in the same direction. When the crunch time comes you feel like you're just not prepared for it. We never had a chance, dealing with all this stupidity on the side.'

After retiring from international cricket, Shuja went public with his complaints, writing that what was needed was 'not only a transformation of the organisation but also a change in culture, stronger staff skills, better performance management and visible leadership'. By now, many of his team-mates were also at the end of their tether. Former captain Orlando Baker told *Cricinfo* in November 2014: 'You can't be coming into a high-profile tournament with only two days of preparation. For players young and old, there's no structure. From a USACA perspective, they don't care.'

Wicketkeeper Akeem Dodson backed him up, saying on social media: 'This administration has failed in team selection, preparation and management. They have failed every touring staff from captain to cook because of their constant refusal to invest in proper team preparation and management prior to departure from American shores.'

But by then the wheels had been set in motion for change at last at the top of the US game. Within weeks the ICC would suspend USACA for a third time and this time there would be no way back.

6

Dreamers and Schemers

'There are too many of these cricket moguls
who want to be rich. They want to be Lalit
Modi. And they see an IPL in the United
States as their ticket to being Modi. That's
what they want to reproduce here and it leads
to bad decision-making.'

Jamie Harrison, American Cricket Federation

EVERY AMERICAN has a dream. It's a birthright endowed not just to every man and woman born in the States, but also those who moved there, who made an active choice to be Americans. Indeed, it's often migrants who dream harder and stronger than those born within the 50 states. Having bought into the idea of America, they are all too often uncynical, oblivious to the unfairness and exploitation that drives unfettered free market capitalism and how the odds are invariably stacked against them.

Every migrant is presented with a question – to what extent do you assimilate? Do you throw yourself unguarded into the melting pot? Or retain a little piece of the old country in your new life? For migrants from South Asia and the Caribbean, one way of maintaining their identity is through cricket.

We have already seen how US cricket has what you might term a weak centre: USACA, a perennially cash-strapped governing body officiated by amateurs. But that weakness is a double-edged sword. The lack of strong direction (and funding) from a governing body, and its location within an entrepreneurial society, has seen US cricket populated by a preponderance of cricket promoters, schemers and dreamers. Driven by their passion, and an often unstated desire 'to give something back' to the sport they remember from their youth, they come up with vehicles to sell, promote or enhance the game. Or at least try to.

Some of them have got off the ground, many didn't. All were fuelled by a fervent hope that cricket could one day flourish in the United States and (though few would admit to it) a hunch that a pot of gold could be just around the corner.

During the course of our travels, we met quite a few of them.

Major League Cricket – the first attempt

Long before the giants of the IPL invested in the US (see chapter 11) there was a man named Bernard Cameron, who registered 'Major League Cricket' as a company back in 2000. A bespectacled, bohemian-looking Trinidadian who had seen the world as a musician before he had made his money on Wall Street, we met him in his office in Brooklyn in November 2005.

It was an exciting time for Cameron. A few weeks later he would launch a new tournament in Florida with six teams representing the states of Florida, North Carolina, Texas, Washington, Pennsylvania and Virginia. This would be known as the Sir Clive Lloyd Cup and Cameron had inveigled the ex-West Indies captain into supporting his project – surely having a West Indies legend as a mascot would imbue Major League Cricket with a patina of respectability?

The major league itself was supposed to have commenced in 2007, with eight teams based on states. There was talk of a programme for youth cricket, National Cricket Centres, a major league coaching certification, umpire's certification, a National Cricket Academy and a goal of developing a team that could qualify for the 2011 World Cup. Big plans. None of which ever came to fruition. But when we met Cameron, he was personable and convincing. And like so many of his kind, dismissive of USACA.

'Over three years, even four years, we have tried to work with USACA to no avail,' he insisted, shaking his head. 'As a matter of fact, when Major League Cricket was formed back in 2000 our first order of business was to get a meeting with USACA and that is when we brought in Clive Lloyd. Clive gave a keynote address to the USACA. So we brought this to them and frankly it was like beating a dead dog. We brought marketing companies, we brought sports marketing entities, we brought stadium restructuring plans.'

With his financial contacts Cameron had brought a construction firm to a meeting with Disney, who then pledged 30 to 40 acres of land in Florida to build a dual-use stadium for cricket and soccer. Cameron was able to get Bear Stearns to agree finance as long as Disney were on board. The final piece of the jigsaw was to get the agreement of USACA. But they did not even deign to provide Cameron with a response.

'At the time I was still working on Wall Street and my company was handling Disney's portfolio,' he shrugs. 'So it was a very embarrassing situation.

'I mean, how could they not respond? It was embarrassing for me not in the sense of USACA but where cricket in America is concerned. I'm selling cricket to these people! So they might invest in the potential development of the game with projected future returns on their investment. I think they [USACA] saw Major League as a threat, instead of looking at it as an opportunity.'

After that humiliation Cameron dusted himself down and went back to the drawing board. He waited until 2005, when he returned with new plans.

'I understand all the issues about the protocol of the ICC, of the governing bodies,' he affirms. But there isn't anything in New York state government and federal government that tells me I can't run a cricket company, and I can't develop cricket in the US. And if, after everything we've done, USACA get the credit for it and cricket is where it's supposed to be, then I'm happy too.'

There was a barely concerned frustration raging beneath his cool exterior. 'There is an old saying: "God grant me the serenity to accept the things I cannot change and courage to change the things I can." Well, I believe that I can change this. This is the difference. I am persistent and the most persistent always win.'

Cameron fervently believed that he could sell cricket to the American public. 'In mainstream America, people talk about "Oh, America is not going to like cricket." That's a fallacy. America is a sports-loving country – period. It's all about the presentation, that's all.

'Education is the key. We just haven't put in place the mechanisms and the infrastructure to educate them about the game! Until we do they will continue to make jokes about the little things they do know – [he puts on a doddery voice] "Oh that old English game, you play for five days and nobody wins." But of course, they have not been educated about the intricacies of the game, the science of the game. They love statistics – cricket is going to be a hit from a statistics perspective!'

When asked about how he would go about selling the game, he became even more animated: 'Number one is access, giving them access. It's going to be a multi-pronged public relations development, marketing – all of the above. So the combination of buzz – what's happening over there, why are there so many people acting so crazy about this sport? What is this sport? Let me go see this sport. So, public relations buzz. Let's take the West Indies players' association team, take an MLC US national team, put them together, take a couple of artists and create an event and take the *Sentinel* down here, bring the *Miami Herald* down here, bring all of the emissaries who are involved in cricket in Florida, all the council generals and they start asking questions.'

To be fair to Cameron, his initial event in November 2005 was a success. In that it actually happened. Flushed by this, Cameron decided that the time was right to go for broke and in February 2006 he wrote to the ICC suggesting that MLC replace USACA as the governing body for cricket in the US.

The ICC considered the request and turned it down, maintaining (at least at this stage) that it could not intervene in domestic governing systems. Cameron was enraged, telling *Cricinfo* that 'it's almost like getting a pardon from the governor after committing murder in a re-election year'.

From here on Cameron and MLC lapsed into silence. Its planned inaugural season in 2007 did not take place and by the following year its website had vanished into the ether too. If MLC was a threat then it was one USACA saw off with comparative ease.

The US Cricket Promoters Association

A few weeks after we met Bernard Cameron, our paths crossed with the United States Cricket Promoters Association in New York. The name might have conjured up a mental image of a slick PR operation, bursting with ideas of how to grow the game and open up new markets. The reality, as we soon discovered, was somewhat different.

The main driving force behind the Promoters Association was a Jamaican gentleman, then in his 71st year called Roy Sweeney. Joining us, when we met him at a hotel lobby not far from JFK, was his younger colleague Peter Jolly, a slightly bumptious fellow who very much played

Robin to Sweeney's Batman. Sweeney radiated a seen-it-all hard-won wisdom; Jolly was an enthusiastic cheerleader, content to defer to his older friend. Neither of them seemed to have much time for Bernard Cameron.

'He's a joke,' scoffed Jolly.

'A dreamer, a big dreamer,' added Sweeney.

The Promoters Association had been formed back in 1986 with the initial aim of organising a match in New York for the full West Indies Test team. 'It was a tremendous success,' Sweeney smiles. 'When I mentioned that I wanted to bring the West Indies Test team over, they laughed at me. "Are you crazy? These guys are not going to come here to play cricket!"

'So I caught a flight to London with a friend of mine from a radio station here, because I wanted him to report back to America that this was being done. We booked into the Cavendish Hotel in London where the team was staying and next morning I went up to Clive Lloyd's door and went "bam bam bam". I said, "I'm here, Clive!" He said, "What are you doing here?" "I want to bring a team to New York." He phoned round the rest of the players and got them to come down and everybody was so delighted to come to New York.'

But recalling the past isn't what they were focusing on in 2005. Their latest project was to build a cricket stadium on the site of Floyd Bennett in Brooklyn, a disused airfield that had recently started to be used as a cricket field. Sweeney had something of a track record on this, and had liaised with a succession of the city's elected mayors to improve cricket facilities at Canarsie and Erskine Fields in Brooklyn.

A stadium was another matter entirely and, during the course of the afternoon, the pair showed us the architect's plans and outlined their vision.

'We'll have the first ICC-approved facility in the United States,' enthused Jolly. 'The cricket field itself will meet the international standards as well as the proper facilities – bleachers, bathrooms, a parking lot, public facilities. It'll be the first of its kind in the United States. We call it Lord's. This will be our Lord's! In the United States!

'We're also going to put a turf wicket, the first one in the USA. We'll put a banqueting hall in place so that during the off-season the other teams and the community can have functions so that we can maintain the field properly. We foresee Floyd Bennett being the mecca of cricket in the world.

'They will come here for their enjoyment, entertainment, recreation and most of all good cricket. In not too far in the immediate future I can see this happening. It's right around the corner, right around the corner … we're looking for investors who understand what's happening and when they take their shares and invest their money they will see many returns because … it's New York. That's what it's all about! That's where the money is. That's where the megabucks are!'

Their problem was twofold: money and politics. Sweeney and co had no real money to speak of and no track record in securing the sort of multi-million-dollar funding it takes to get a project of this scale off the ground. The Promoters Association were looking for investors who shared their vision. It didn't help that they didn't have the backing of the national body. USACA – as was their wont – had kept Sweeney at arm's length, to his intense irritation.

'I have been involved in cricket here for decades – nobody has my track record! Nobody. Not USACA. Nobody. And they have never invited me to one of their meetings. Here is a guy who has done great things, has great ideas – these are the kind of people you want to work with! Let's invite him to one of our meetings and hear what he has to say.'

Perhaps still thinking it's based in London, he asks us whether we know anyone at the ICC. We don't.

(By bizarre coincidence, in Joseph O'Neill's *Netherland* there is a passage in which Chuck Ramkissoon, the cricket entrepreneur, takes the novel's narrator Hans down to Floyd Bennett and tells him of his dream to build a cricket stadium there. Ramkissoon's exact words are eerily similar to the ones Sweeney uses during our interview in 2005. We later mention this to O'Neill when we meet him, but he swears blind that he had never met Roy Sweeney. Not knowingly, anyway. A spooky coincidence? Or fact and fiction intertwining?)

Once it becomes clear to him that our address books don't contain any juicy connections at the ICC, Sweeney's mood becomes more melancholic. He talks of how he migrated to the States from Jamaica when he was just 17, the sacrifices he's made. 'When I came here all of my thoughts were, "Gosh, I wonder if they play cricket here?" and finally when I found out that they did play cricket here I got involved!

'My wife hates me. My kids hate me. Tremendous sacrifice! I have pumped a lot of money into cricket. But it's sometimes a nightmare. I leave the cricket field and I go home and my wife is like, "Don't touch me. Go back to your cricketers." It's a tremendous price we pay to make sure that cricket is being played here. I have two sons and they don't want to hear about cricket! They were born here. Very few people love cricket as much as I do.'

His mind drifts back to 1986 and that first West Indies game in New York: 'I couldn't believe it – the first day I got up at 8.30 in the morning and I got my driver up, gets me and the players together for breakfast. And when we pull up at the park people were lined up for about two miles for their cricket.

'I couldn't believe it. There were not enough seats. People stood around. We got some sponsors – Guinness Gold. We were given 500 cases of beer by Guinness Gold. Every bottle of beer was gone at two dollars a bottle! The food was all sold out by 2.30! Every supermarket in the area, everything was gone. Sunday was worse! And this is not a dream that I've had – this is something that I've experienced!'

Some dreams come true. Most don't. The stadium never happened. But Sweeney did get to relive his finest moment in 2006 when he organised one more game in New York for a West Indies XI that included Chris Gayle, Shivnarine Chanderpaul and Brian Lara. He died in April 2013 aged 78 but lived long enough to see his contributions to the game in the US officially recognised when he was awarded the ICC Centenary Medal in 2010.

And if one day that stadium at Floyd Bennett is ever built, one hopes it will be named in his honour.

Lloyd Jodah and American College Cricket

June 2014. As soon as we meet him in an Upper West Side cafe, Lloyd Jodah is adamant about one thing: he is an American.

'Any description of me has to be "American". And not "expatriate" either. I don't use the word. I don't like it applied to me,' he insists. 'Now, of course, I grew up in the Caribbean, so my cricket pedigree is West Indian, my ethnic background is Indian. But I chose to be American, and I am proud of that. One of the biggest weaknesses with people who try to do anything with cricket in the United States is that they come to it with a foreign perspective.'

He's a lively, opinionated presence; one, you sense, with a bit of an ego. Within the US cricket scene, Jodah has rubbed many people up the wrong way and runs his project very much as a personal fiefdom. However, unlike others, it has maintained a constant presence for over a decade and a half and Jodah is nothing if not proud of the difference he's made: 'We've had over 2,000 people playing the game. Some of those people are having their best memories playing American College Cricket.'

Jodah was a cricket junkie (another one) from an early age, even claiming that he was playing the game before he was able to walk. And like the others he claims he's had a calling: 'I thought it was such a pity that such a great game was making no headway in the United States. You see these guys playing in leagues which are basically recreational leagues, without a clue about what it takes to move the game forward. My goal was to change that and raise the profile of the game. I figured, "Nobody else is doing it so I should do it!" It was as straightforward as that.'

He spent some time researching his options, before deciding to invest in the college game. 'It was obvious. If you look at different American sports, the grassroots for American sports is not what cricketers commonly think is grassroots, which is elementary schools. No, it's college. Every single major American sport has come out of college and it has developed up and down, up to the professional, down to the other levels. It's a totally unique structure and nobody in the cricket world gets that.

'The very first competitive American football game was Rutgers v Princeton in 1869. All of these sports came out of college. They have the resources to pour into it, they have reasons to get more publicity. And of course they have brand names as well, so they lend power, right? So I decided this is a no-brainer! We can bring the brand name of these colleges to cricket! It's our best chance of going somewhere fast.'

Jodah had to finance the 2007 debut season largely by himself. Registration fees for teams were set deliberately low. 'For the first year it couldn't be much, because I was basically asking a bunch of random guys to fund themselves to come to Florida. So to add an onerous registration fee would have been too much, right?'

Launching it in the Sunshine State was a smart move. 'It was Fort Lauderdale at spring break. So it's perfect – beaches, lots of nightlife. Remember I'm trying to motivate guys in their early 20s to come and spend their money and play cricket. Basically, I'm saying, "Instead of spending your money and just getting drunk, you can come down here." You can come and party and play cricket.'

The initial tournament caught the attention of the *New York Times*, who sent a reporter down to Fort Lauderdale to cover it, a fact that Jodah mentions several times during our conversation. After the initial year the league grew up to the point where over 90 colleges are taking part.

In terms of demographics, the league is dominated by players from a South Asian background. '90% Indian,' says Jodah, 'and I'd say around 50% of those will be international students.' But all are encouraged and indeed the league has an annual award for the best player from a non-cricketing background, named after America's greatest ever cricketer John Bart King.

'That first story in the *New York Times* really did a lot for the game in the US,' he boasts. 'It's been one of the keys to what I'm doing, because the cricket community outside of American College Cricket don't understand it. It's like two different worlds right now – American College Cricket and the rest of cricket in this country. But I spend no time being negative about what they're doing. I mean, there is no acknowledgement of what I'm doing. But I never make a comment. You won't see me bad-mouthing them.'

He's right in that there is a disconnect between his project and the cricketing mainstream in the US. When we ask if there is a route for the kids to join a club after they finish college, Jodah talks around the subject.

And College Cricket is not without its controversies. The scoring system for the league is somewhat eccentric, with 'spirit' points being awarded for off-the-field activities.

Jodah explains: 'From the early days I gave them points for off-the-field performance as well, which has to do with promoting of the game. For example, if you're able to get an article in your school media – I tell people I'd much rather have an article on a school website than a cricket website because my goal is to spread the game beyond cricket people, right? I said once in an interview with a Canadian radio station that I'd rather be on a college website than *Cricinfo* and they edited it out!

'So it's stuff like that, or if you have a table at a sports fair where you had cricket equipment or you come and talk to people about cricket and demonstrate it. Anything that helps get the game beyond just playing it, right?'

Posting on social media counts too. Indeed, according to Jodah, it played a pivotal role in getting his project off the ground in the first place. 'In 2008 there was nobody really promoting cricket on Facebook, before I did it. *Cricinfo* didn't even have a Facebook page back then!

'For me it was simple. How do I find the guys who are playing cricket? Obviously at that time Facebook was still primarily a college medium. So this is where I find them. I got on Facebook and started my profile. I had no clue how to use it – I had to teach myself. Basically, I started reaching out to guys and if they made a comment it would say your university affiliation. So I would know this was a college student, right?

'So I sent a friend request, but of course I have to give an explanation. Because imagine if you're a college student and some random guy sends you a friend request. That doesn't look too good, does it? Why is this weirdo sending me a friend request? So I had to explain, "I'm the president of American College Cricket and I plan to stage a national championship."'

The other controversy is that at national championships no food and water is provided for the players. This has led to online tales about parched and hungry young cricketers wilting in the heat after a long day's play, and much criticism of Jodah's whole project.

'We never provide food,' he protests. 'We never have done. It's just not practical. The logistics of getting all the different dietary requirements right for 4,000 people …

can you imagine what would happen if we got that wrong? We always provide water, though. Maybe the people complaining on that day did not receive any.'

It's at this point that our tape runs out. I reach for my bag for a replacement and suddenly Jodah becomes agitated. Despite the fact that we had earlier indicated to him that we would be taping the conversation, he clearly has forgotten or not heard. He protests and agrees to continue only on the understanding that he is not recorded.

Despite his protestations that he is an American, Jodah didn't appear from nowhere. Like many of America's cricketing entrepreneurs, he is an immigrant, a Guyanese whose parents knew many of the island's cricketing elite. With some prompting the memories start to flow.

'I grew up around top-class players, I know class when I see it! When I was a boy for instance I used to wake up Alvin Kallicharran, and I'd run with him around the field, bowl at him in the nets. He was my uncle – not by blood though.

'Every single Indian guy who was a batsman, whether they played Test cricket or first-class cricket, passed through our place, because we lived in the city. So in order to play the top-level cricket they had to come to the city. They would stay with us, because my father and his brothers were extremely generous. Ridge Road in Guyana – it's one of the most illustrious addresses in world cricket and nobody knows about it! Even Shiv Chanderpaul – he used to spend three or four days a week there.'

And with that our conversation ends. But in 2024 US College Cricket is still going strong. For all his eccentricities, Jodah's scheme has meant that thousands of students have been able to play the game they love and that can only be seen in a positive light.

Venu Palaparthi and Dream Cricket

How can I contribute? That is the question that all the figures in this chapter have asked themselves. Loving the game so much and seeing the state of it in their adoptive country, they have taken JFK's famous plea and adapted it: 'Ask not what US cricket can do for you, but what you can do for US cricket.'

Venu Palaparthi runs Dreamcricket.com. For over 20 years and through various incarnations it's been the go-to online portal about the sport Stateside. And whilst *Cricinfo* and the governing body's website get more online traffic from the US, Dreamcricket is a vital platform. If it were ever to disappear, American cricket would undoubtedly be the poorer for its absence.

'From its very start Dreamcricket has always kind of given money away,' Palaparthi shrugs. 'It even continues to this day. It comes with the territory. You're in America, you can't make money out of cricket! You could probably make money out of cricket if you're a massive distributor and there were some times when we did make some money. But we give away more money than we make, to this day. The goal always was to be a loss leader and build a footprint, so to that extent we've been successful.'

We're talking in an Indian restaurant on New York's Upper West Side in late 2018, coincidentally slap bang next to a bar named Manhattan Cricket Club. Dream Cricket started out as a fantasy cricket league site, launching just before the 1999 World Cup. Venu had already started writing for it and was asked to take it over in 2004. 'I gave it a really new spin. I said, "We can't sustain the hosting costs, the infrastructure costs involved in maintaining this. We're doing it because we care about cricket and love the sport."

'Most reasonable start-ups have a commercial goal to make money eventually and in our case I would say it has been deferred by about … 20 years now.' He laughs out loud. 'For 18 years we have not made money. But we have had some revenue streams that have been pretty good.'

Initially one was selling DVDs, the 2005 Ashes series and *Richie Benaud's Greatest XI* being some of the most popular, before online streaming killed that market. Luckily before then they had started selling cricket gear on the site.

'Naively, we bought $4,000 worth of Gunn and Moore equipment, thinking it will take about a year to sell this. Over 70% of it had gone in the space of two months, so then we started selling more stuff. We became distributors of MRF and Kookaburra. When I say "distributors" that's kind of glorified. What it means is that we were buying $10,000 worth of equipment and selling it over time.'

But selling equipment tends to be seasonal and the site was still losing money. Then Venu had the brainwave of diversifying into online league management – in other words scorekeeping and online administration for the various cricket leagues dotted around the country.

'We started signing up leagues – we had about 15 in the end. Again, we were doing it for free so why would you say no? We got more and more people coming in, without a tremendous sense of loyalty or anything. So they wouldn't buy anything from us. They would just use our system, but they would be able to feed this machine.'

In the midst of all this Dreamcricket also launched an indoor facility – batting cages – in Newark, New Jersey and even tried to get their own T20 tournament off the ground. 'We made it city-based so it was New Jersey, New York, Washington DC, Philadelphia, Boston. There were six teams. We did it for three years. Each year the quality improved but we couldn't scale it because at some point there are only so many tents you can put in, chairs you can rent and parking spots you could negotiate with the township because cricket grounds are not ideally located.'

Whilst the indoor facility lost money, Venu had started noticing more and more parents bringing their kids in to use it. 'I said, "Maybe we should take these kids and do something with them." So we brought a coach from India and we announced a summer camp. First year we had four kids and that was the start of the Dream Cricket Academy.'

The indoor facility was closed, the league and league management side closed down and the site concentrated on its role as a news portal, with the academy and advertising keeping things afloat, though Venu admits to being tempted to open another indoor facility. At present the academy has two under-12 youth teams, two each at under-14 and under-16 levels and one under-18 side. Two graduates of the academy ended up turning out for the US national under-19 team.

He admits the whole project is a write-off. Working on Wall Street, he can afford it. 'It's an expensive hobby. It operates on the generosity of its sponsors and my own interest. I've probably spent over $1million on this. But it allows me to exercise my writing skills. I'm probably the only one who has written about US cricket for the entire length of time. I've been going about 14 years.'

'I think we have been an independent voice and continue to be that independent voice. The ecosystem for cricket did not exist so we kind of naively believed that we could create it – if you build it they will come. We've built it, even though we had to shut down some pieces and build it again. But at least it still exists, and people appreciate it.'

Most of the characters we met had big dreams, dreams that couldn't become reality due to a lack of money, organisation or by the very fact they were working on a part-time basis. Dream Cricket is different in that Venu had very modest ambitions and has over 20 years maintained a constant presence on a constantly changing landscape. 'We kind of quickly realised that the best approach is the pragmatic one so over time we did re-calibrate it,' smiles Venu as he finishes his meal. 'It's taken a toll – believe me, it's not easy.'

Like so many he's driven by a deep, unfathomable and enduring love. 'For me it's just … somebody has to do it! Sounds clichéd but 20 dollars is what I came in with. My wife thinks I might be stupid enough to blow all my money on this, but I still got to do it.'

Jamie Harrison, the United States Youth Cricket Association and the American Cricket Federation

As Gladstone Dainty's vice-like grip on USACA entered a second decade and the incompetence and dismal standard of administration of the game in the US became ever more notorious, voices began to call for a breakaway.

Jamie Harrison is unlike anyone else featured in this chapter. His dreams weren't fuelled by expat reveries or nostalgia for a supposed cricketing 'golden age'. He is a white American whose family has lived in Maryland since the 1670s. A high school teacher by profession, he knew nothing about the game until he took his class to a Civil War site in Virginia one day.

'They were demonstrating cricket as an artefact of America's past,' he recalled when we met him in Baltimore in 2014. 'I had some teenage boys with me and at some point we said, "Let's do it." The chaperone got involved, I got involved, we played for about an hour and a half, had a great time. We left and for the rest of the day all they could talk about was cricket. The entire point of the field trip was lost, much to my chagrin. On the way home they kept saying, "We're going to form a cricket club."

'We get back to school and I thought, "Okay, this is the flavour of the week, this will pass." On Monday they are in front of my desk and they said, "We'd like you to be the moderator of our cricket club." And I said, "Okay, there's a problem. We don't have any cricket equipment." They said, "Don't worry Mr Harrison, if you order some with your credit card I'm sure we'll pay you back." I took a flyer and I did it. Then they came to me at the end of the school year and said, "We want to play a proper intra-mural tournament, we want to form teams and have insurance."'

Though not one of Harrison's students had a trace of ancestry among the Test-playing nations, they soon graduated on to hard-ball cricket and started playing matches against other schools. After a difficult start – getting 'annihilated' in their first game – they steadily improved. Then the school closed, for financial reasons. The cricket team was no more and Harrison found himself out of a job.

'At that point I had a decision to make. This cricket thing could be a weird moment in my life that people will laugh about at family gatherings later. Or I can do something with it. Because that one year span had been like a laboratory experiment playing out in front of my very eyes. I'd always been told Americans don't understand cricket, Americans will not play cricket. But I watched American boys go from knowing nothing to playing hard-ball cricket against experienced kids and enjoying it and competing. And I thought, "If I can replicate that in other schools – and by replicate I mean just introduce them to the game and leave behind a classic cricket set for them to play with – I bet kids would like it."'

So Harrison contacted Venu and Dreamcricket.com. 'He said he'd donate ten plastic cricket sets if we took them to Maryland schools and let him know what happens. So I did and everywhere I went the kids fell in love with the game. The teachers loved it because it was different. They were so sick of the same sports over and over again. The kids wanted something new, the teachers wanted something new. The kids loved it because it was hitting and running and high-scoring.'

So Harrison upped the ante to 100 sets and started supplying entire school systems. Then using social media he made a video of himself and, explaining the concept, asked if anyone else wanted to get involved. 'Then a guy in Kansas contacted me who said, "I've been doing this in Kansas for years, but USACA refuses to support it." I had a guy in Connecticut who said, "I want to be involved" and before you knew it the Maryland Youth Cricket Association had become the United States Youth Cricket Association [USYCA} and we had little bastions all over the country.'

By 2014 Harrison had given away over 1,500 cricket sets and the USYCA had over 16 member organisations. 'I've crunched the numbers, looked at the schools' totals and enrolment and thought, "If 25% of them touched a cricket bat during the course of the year that's probably the best I could hope for." Based on those numbers we've probably engaged with 50,000–75,000 kids over the last few years.'

That in itself would constitute an admirable contribution to the development of the game in the US, but in the midst of all this Harrison also got himself involved in the creation of a new governing body: the American Cricket Federation.

The catalyst was the blatant gerrymandering that went on in the (themselves delayed) 2012 USACA elections. As we saw in chapter 4, 32 leagues were overnight ruled as 'non-compliant' by Gladstone Dainty. Twenty of those leagues met, drafted a new constitution and Harrison threw USYCA in with them.

'It was basically a reaction to the tyranny of USACA. We created the anti-USACA – an incredibly representative system that includes voting members from all facets of the cricketing public, term limits ... all the protections you can imagine that would come from people who had experienced the tyranny of a few.'

The first ACF elections were held in September 2013 and Harrison found himself its first CEO. The next step, he explained, was to win over the ICC.

'I received ICC paperwork today,' he says proudly. 'It shows the agenda for the annual meeting in Melbourne that is coming up and USACA is going to be put on notice, that they are out of compliance. It's rule 3.1, which says that you have to demonstrate that you are the sole governing body for cricket in your nation and clearly they are not. We are a parallel governing body. So they are going to be put on notice at the meeting next week and they will be given 12 months to rectify the non-compliance. And 12 months hence, if they have not rectified it – which they won't – they will be suspended at next year's annual meeting. Twelve months after that, if the both of us still exist, the US will be expelled from the ICC.'

And yet minutes after telling us this, Harrison is adamant the ACF doesn't need ICC recognition at all. 'The past challenges to USACA have all been predicated on the idea that they have to be recognised by the ICC and get ICC money to be successful. Their entire model is, "We're going to convince the ICC to take the national governing body status from USACA and give it to us." And if that doesn't happen, everything falls apart.

'We can live without the ICC. I would like to have their partnerships, but it's not necessary. I think they are eventually going to want to be associated with us, more so than we are going to need to be associated with them ...'

In the meantime the ACF was going ahead with their T20 tournament and on the day we met him Harrison had just bagged a sponsorship deal with Newbery. But he seemed an impatient man and one wondered whether he would have the forbearing and tenacity required to see what would inevitably be a long-term project through to its completion. Towards the end of our conversation, he admitted as much:

'What I worry about myself sometimes is that I'm so hyper-aggressive and so into it and so focused that I'm going to burn out and I'm not going to make it to the end. So I do have to take a breath sometimes and think of the long haul.

'There are moments when I sit back and I say to myself: "You're trying to change the cricket culture of a modern industrialised nation!" Then I have to stop. Because if you get caught up in that it will become daunting and you'll become more easily discouraged.'

It was a prescient moment of reflection. Less than 12 months later Harrison had resigned as the CEO and returned to focus on his role as head of the US Youth Cricket Association. 'I was never a true CEO in the way in which, say, Microsoft has a CEO,' he admitted. 'I am more Che Guevara than Satya Nadella, more community organiser than boardroom suit.'

In truth by that point, the ACF was also struggling to live up to Harrison's bold aims. Their 2014 inter-league championships included a number of forfeited games as teams struggled to travel for matches out of state and by 2015 the number of competing teams had dropped from 17 to 13. Money was also a problem – monies generated during the period 2014/15 amounted to less than $50,000.

Eventually, Harrison got his wish. The ICC did intervene and USACA were expelled. But as we shall we see later on in this journey, the ACF were not to be the beneficiaries.

7

'Just Play More'

The growing pains of US women's cricket

IF MEN'S cricket in America has often seemed to be in a state of arrested development, its undoubted potential thwarted by issues of scale, funding and amateurism, spare a thought for their female counterparts. In terms of status, organisation and mere presence, the women's game lags some way behind even their hapless menfolk. Indeed, up until a decade or so ago it could realistically be described as barely existing at all, beyond a loose cluster of pioneer figures that have, with gritted teeth and sheer determination, kept the flame flickering in their own local areas.

These pioneers haven't waited for USACA or the ICC to do the right thing and make a financial commitment to developing the women's game. They have just got on with it, often in the face of indifference, poverty and the time constraints of everyday family life (not to mention the odd bit of old-fashioned misogyny). On this odyssey we have been looking for that intangible yet unmistakable 'spirit of cricket'. If anybody can be said to be imbued with it, it's the ordinary women who have kept the game alive in the States over the last few decades.

They have received little or no support from the men purporting to govern cricket in the US. As far as USACA were concerned they were not a priority. Indeed, it wasn't until the ICC mandated that associate nations had to have a women's programme in place by 2015 that the body appointed someone to oversee this process. And it was a man: John Aaron, the grandee of the Atlantis club in the New York region, who, as secretary, had been Gladstone Dainty's number two for three years from 2008, who was appointed to oversee this.

'There weren't that many advocates on the board for women's cricket,' he explained to us when we spoke to him in 2011. 'Yes, there were board members who felt we wanted to have women's cricket, but since the resources are so limited and the personnel is so limited, the focus clearly has been on men's cricket. I have, along with some others, tried to advocate for women's cricket and in fact it is the president's wish right now to have a woman on the USACA board, if only to advocate and to represent on behalf of women's cricket. That's quite rightly so. That's the way it should be.'

Aaron, to be fair, is an ally of the women's game, and did his best with the meagre resources at his disposal. Back in 2011 there weren't just any women's leagues in the US, there were barely any teams. Aaron estimated that there were enough women playing the game to make up two teams in the New York region, three in California and one in the New Jersey/Maryland/Baltimore seaboard. Six teams in the entire country.

All of which makes the national team's achievement in reaching the Women's World Cup qualifiers in Bangladesh that year all the more extraordinary. Nadia Gruny was an opening batter and looks back fondly on that time, describing it as 'the best experience the national team has had to date'.

Nadia's story is similar to many from that team. Originally from Tobago, she came to the US to study, arriving at South Carolina State University, interestingly, on a soccer scholarship. She went on to study for a Masters in Sports Business Management and was only reintroduced to the sport when, as part of the course, she found herself doing an internship at a men's club in Georgia. Up until that point she'd had no idea there was any possibility of trying her hand at the sport in her adopted country.

The US team had been put together post-2009, after the ICC's intervention. With no leagues or any way of measuring cricketing talent a call was put out to the nation's female cricketers to try out for the national squad. Many former West Indies players found themselves in the team, figures like Roselyn Emmanuel and Shirley-Ann Bonaparte.

The US were in a regional qualifying group with Canada, Brazil, Bermuda and Argentina. When the US and Canada finished joint top, a three-game ODI play-off decided who would go to Bangladesh, which the US won 3-0.

Nadia remembers the culture shock. 'It was the first real international tour for us. We were among some really strong teams like the West Indies, Sri Lanka, Pakistan, Bangladesh and it was way above our level. And not only that but we went into that tournament with not our full-strength team. One of our best players couldn't make it because she was a pilot. Another player got pregnant. So the team that eventually went to Bangladesh was far from our first-strength team. And of course, we didn't have the depth to be able to field a decent second-strength side.'

In typical USACA style there were also financial issues. 'When we went to Canada in the summer earlier that year the stipend that we were given was pretty standard compared to what the men got,' remembers Gruny. 'But then when we went to Bangladesh there was a significant decrease to the stipend they were offering. And so whilst there was never any change with the men they [USACA] made the argument that, "Well, it's Bangladesh so things are cheaper there.'"

Inevitably, preparations were far from ideal. Linden Fraser, the coach that had successfully got them through the regional qualifiers, was dismissed shortly before the tournament to make way for ex-India international Robin Singh. When the squad arrived in Bangladesh, they discovered that not only had USACA neglected to arrange any practice matches, they hadn't even bothered to sort out anywhere to train. 'We got there and found out that the first day or first couple of days we had to use the tennis courts at the hotel to practise.'

The girls lost every game except one: a nail-biting finish against Zimbabwe at the Sher-a-Bangla stadium in Mirpur that was televised, another first for the team. The US had set their opponents 188. But with one over and one wicket remaining Zimbabwe needed just two runs to win. 'They were on their last wicket and just decided to go for this run or two runs that was absolutely not necessary and Shebani [Bhaskar] had a direct hit at the wicket.

'Oh my gosh! You'd swear that we'd won the whole event. Everyone just ran and screamed and jumped and it was just pure elation. Unbelievable. I just couldn't imagine that our team had won a game and over a full member!

I mean, granted it's Zimbabwe, but for us it was such a massive win.'

It should have been a platform, a starting point for the US women's team to grow and develop over the coming decade. Instead it was an end. When the next T20 qualifiers came round in 2012 the US team went out to Canada. But there was worse to come. The low participation level for women's cricket in the region meant that ICC Americas pulled the funding for international tournaments indefinitely. The US team, and indeed women cricketers all over the Americas, were left high and dry.

'We lost a decade,' is Nadia's summary. Without any international fixtures to aim towards, without any sort of league structure or any clubs, women were forced to rely on their own resources – themselves – to keep the game alive. 'Between 2012 and 2015 was extremely painful,' she laments. 'Those were four years, which would have been critical in helping to advance the game in the US.

'But during that time some of us tried not to lose heart. We still played cricket locally. We played with the men, especially in California. We got the support of one of the local leagues and they assembled a female team. Many times the team would comprise boys or men if we couldn't field a full XI on the day. But it was such a fantastic opportunity for us and I can vouch for that myself, because we played two full seasons and we had never done that before.'

On the other side of the country another woman was making plans. Petal Samuels is a Guyanese who emigrated to the States in the 1990s, making her home in Georgia. In 2010, she had played in a women's tournament organised in Florida with a team called New Jersey Spirit. 'When I asked them where we were going next year nobody had a definitive answer so I said, "Come to Georgia and I will host a women's tournament." At that time I was playing with Metropolitan Cricket Club in Lithonia so when I got back home I contacted them and friends who I knew had some money in the bank and told them, "Listen, let's have a women's tournament in Georgia in 2011."'

Petal was flying by the seat of her pants. 'Here I am, never hosted anything like this before and never knowing the finer details about how to organise the tournament. But fortunately, I had men like John Aaron to guide me on how to get it done.

'We invited five teams but only one and a half teams showed up. No matter. I was just jumping for joy to see women playing in Georgia. At that time we had never had a women's team playing in Georgia, let alone a whole tournament.'

Petal also experienced some resistance from the local male players. 'Some of them could be heard saying, "We need not be on the field – it's a gentlemen's sport. We should go back to the kitchen and just make the tea, to not be on the field." But the women who came out and played, they gave it their all and they actually converted the sceptics into believers. I was happy that the women came out and played so hard that the men believed in us. We still get a bit of that from them but it's not as loud as before!'

Since then the Georgia tournament has grown with teams coming from further afield including the Cayman Islands, Canada and players from New Zealand, Uganda, Zimbabwe and, on one occasion, Peru. The West Indies captain Stephanie Taylor even popped in to make a guest appearance one year.

But Petal was only just getting started. She knew that in order to survive the Atlanta tournament couldn't just be a one woman show, so she created the Georgia Women's Cricket Association as a governing body for the tournament. 'Of course, all the positions are voluntary,' she notes. 'When I started I didn't think we needed all of that but as I grew in knowledge and understanding of how these things worked I realised that things like the IPL have a whole structure behind them that runs the tournament.'

In addition to this she also became a certified Level 1 coach with Cricket Australia and a certified West Indies umpire. The GWCA has also spent time trying to get cricket into schools in Georgia. A proper league is the next step and indeed Samuels had plans to put that in place, but they were stymied by the pandemic and ensuing pause to all forms of cricket.

As anyone who organises grassroots sport will nod in recognition, Petal's is a tiring and demanding job without much reward. 'It feels lonely and I will admit to you that I have cried many days and many nights because you get the backlash. "Who is Petal Samuels? Petal Samuels has never played for any team, she never played for the US national team and where is she getting all this money from to do this?"

'There have been many times where a particular person might say, "Call me back on Friday. I'll give you the sponsorship that I promised you." And I will keep calling back and they would not answer their phone. And others who say, "Yes" they're going to sponsor water or Gatorade or whatever it is, sometimes do not come up. So I do have many lonely days and I do cry. But cricket is bigger than me. When I look towards the future of what cricket can be – I remember when soccer was nothing in the US and you see where it is now – I know we have that part to play, so that cricket can be great in this nation. I want a legacy that I have done my part in helping to develop USA women's cricket.'

Petal is not the only one who has tried to make something out of nothing, tried to sow seeds on what many assume is barren land. Julie Abbott is an English expat, who, like many others, assumed her career in the game was over when she emigrated to Kansas City in 1988.

'It was non-existent,' she explains. 'Obviously back in the late 1980s it's not like we had Google or the opportunity to do a quick search to see if there was any women's cricket. There was no women's cricket to my knowledge whatsoever and I understand from being involved now for the past decade or so that it wasn't probably until the 2000s that there was any women's cricket around.'

Abbott had played in England before she emigrated ('I played in the days when we were playing in a skirt so that kind of ages me') and in frustration had taken up golf to keep fit. It would take an unlikely trip to a Chinese restaurant to redirect her towards her first sporting love.

'I was on a business trip coming back from Dallas and as I left my hotel room I grabbed a fortune cookie I had taken the previous evening when we dined out with some Chinese food. So I made a beeline for Fort Worth airport, sat on the plane and opened this fortune cookie. It kind of said that I needed to get back involved with something that I was passionate about in my life. And I remember sitting on the plane thinking that the only thing that I've ever really and truly been 100% passionate about is cricket. Then I Googled "Women's cricket USA Missouri" and learned that there had been a women's national team that past year that had been selected to go out to Bangladesh and participate in a World Cup qualifier.

'I was amazed that I had gone from 1988, on the understanding that there was no cricket, and now there I was in 2012 suddenly realising there was this team of players. But what struck me most was the age of the players and the make-up of that national team. It was all expats – Asian and West Indian women that had landed and found their way, living and working in the States. I think at that time they had a captain who was 42 years of age and obviously for the rest of the competing countries their average age was considerably lower.'

Abbott knew she had to get involved. She reached out to a team in the St Louis/Missouri area that played mixed gender cricket and played a match with them. She undertook a coaching course and was then invited to take part in Petal Samuels's Georgia tournament. She wasted no time in scrabbling together a team of Canadians and Americans, which she dubbed Can-Am.

'We were runners-up in our first tournament,' she explains, 'and I think there were only two players on that team who had any prior knowledge of one another. Everybody else was new to one another. But we had a lot of fun and played, quite frankly, really well. From there we decided that our focus should be "let's go and play more.".

'It was during this time that ICC Americas had determined that there was not enough participation in the Americas in women's cricket and therefore they couldn't continue with any regional competitions. They stopped funding them and obviously this was very frustrating to us. So Can-Am made a business decision that until ICC Americas were back fully fledged with their support for women's cricket that we would take on a role in keeping women's cricket alive in the Americas.'

This was a big task for just one team, but Julie had found her calling. She organised for then-England captain Charlotte Edwards and New Zealand's Suzie Bates to come out and do some coaching. Can-Am held a series of development camps and kept interest up by touring to England in August 2016 (when they played against an MCC team), to Argentina in 2015 and 2016, and to Mexico in November 2018. They also became the first women's team to participate in the Philadelphia Cricket Festival (see chapter 1).

Can-Am undoubtedly played a role to the extent that some even dubbed them the 'MCC of the Americas'. 'We saw our role as just keeping women's cricket alive in the USA,' says Abbott. 'The whole idea was to keep female cricketers engaged, supported and give them opportunities to play more. Our tagline was "just play more" and that was all we were trying to do – provide some opportunities so that it wasn't the same few players having to play against each other all the time.'

There were others too who played a part. Joan Alexander Serrano was a Grenadian international who represented West Indies at Test level. After migrating to the States, she later played for her adopted home and was in the squad for Bangladesh at the age of 50. She founded Legacy International Women Cricketers in 2014, with the idea of bringing youngsters together with older players that are still passionate about the game. 'A lot of older women cricketers are looking for opportunities to pass on their knowledge about the sport they love to the next generation,' she explained at the time. 'We know how much the game has given us and want to give something back to youngsters in the US.' To that end, from 2014 she staged occasional tournaments in the New York and Philadelphia area that provided much-needed opportunities for female players to play.

Even younger players like Nadia Gruny became proactive: 'Around 2014 I also orchestrated a bit of a programme to get some grants from a private non-profit organisation to fund a programme for female cricketers. Because I was pretty sure that at some point cricket was going to return for women, and so we shouldn't just sit and wait for that to happen! I got funding for a simple one-year programme where there were two training camps just over a long weekend.

'That funding also took the team to Trinidad to play some matches. It's funny we played the under-19s Trinidad team just to get the competition level. Actually we won one of them! It was a great experience. The under-19 cricketers in Trinidad were really good – well, they grew up playing cricket, unlike us. So here we are, a bunch of 20- or 30-something women playing cricket against these young kids. So we did things like that to keep ourselves busy and involved with the game.'

The ICC Americas decision and the later expulsion of USACA robbed many players of their best years. Current US captain Sindhu Shriharsha was another migrant who arrived during this time. She had played for India under-21s and India A, but all that was put to one side when she married and relocated to the Bay Area in 2013.

'I still wanted to play,' she explains. 'I Googled "women's cricket, who do I contact?" And I did find two leagues that were already here. One at BACA – Bay Area Cricket Association and there's another one, the Northern California Cricket Association (NCCA). The two big leagues in the Bay Area and both of them had a women's team. Well, it was not a fully women's team. The girls would play along with the youth, the under-16s make up the girls' and the boys' team together to make an XI to play against the men's teams. So I started off that way. Between 2013 and 2015 all I did was play in the men's leagues.

'They would really encourage us and really respected the fact that we were coming out there every week and trying to compete with them. It's not like they were taking it easy or trying to bowl a little slowly. No, they were challenging us. And then we were friends outside. We would finish the game off and then spend time with each other. It was kind of like a whole big family supporting each other.'

* * *

It wasn't until 2017, with the end of the wrangling over the governing body in sight, that the ICC allowed the US women's team to compete in European World Cup qualifiers as a wild card entry. If this was a Hollywood movie there would be a redemptive ending with the USA women overcoming the odds on their return. But this was real life. It was also Scotland in late summer.

'It was horrible! Really horrible,' remembers Nadia. 'We played, I think, a total of two matches in that entire qualifying event because everything else was rained off. We played on the very first day and the very last day and we lost both. We didn't qualify. It was then back to the drawing board.'

But it was a start and with the new governing body a going concern by 2018, further infrastructure could be put in place. A regular programme of camps was instituted. Then in 2019 USA Cricket appointed a head coach for the national team in former Australia wicket-keeper Julia Price.

A two-time World Cup winner who had become the first female to coach a men's team in the Big Bash, Price had achieved everything there was to achieve in women's cricket. And she knew full well what she was taking on and the difficulty of the task that lay ahead.

'Yes, I had been briefed, very much so!' she laughed when we interviewed her in 2020. 'When the opportunity came along, I thought, "Wow, this is a major project." In terms of making the decision to take the job, the clincher was the players themselves. 'They were so excited and so keen to learn and so ready to take on the world. They seemed excited that someone from Australia was interested in them and had turned up at one of their combines and we gave away a few shirts to some of the girls. They were just absolutely stoked, having their photo taken with me all the time and it was really unexpected. I just didn't think it was going to be that big a deal for these girls that I had taken an interest in what they were doing and was actually quite interested in the development of their game.'

That said, even on that first day Price was given an insight into what she was letting herself in for. 'The facilities for training were one of those things where you roll your eyes a little bit. It's supposed to be the national squad and they are on a skinny concrete pitch in the middle of nowhere in San Jose with a couple of dodgy nets on the side which had the bars in so when you hit the ball it deflects back on to your head.

'But that sort of stuff sort of resonated with me. They weren't bitching about it. They were just getting on with it. It is what it is, and I liked that attitude.'

Price's first game was a regional qualifier for the T20 World Cup against Canada, which the USA duly won. It had been the first time the team had studied tactics and analysed the opposition. 'They started to understand that it's not just going out there and hitting the ball. You actually have to have a bit of a plan.' This led them into a global T20 qualifier, which meant a return to Scotland in September 2019.

'We were laughing that it happened to be in the same place, of all the odds. Half the fun is getting a free trip to somewhere exotic!' remembers Erica Rendler, the opener who, as we will see later, is one of the few white native-born Americans to play the sport at this level.

'But it was great. I think I got 46 runs in 30-something balls and still we were disappointed with our wins and losses at the end of it. And the rain! We spent so much time in the locker room drinking tea and having conversations with one another that went on way too long.'

All the team's games were either washed out or lost. Until their final game against Namibia when Nadia Gruny hit 33 to lead a successful run chase, winning by six wickets and thus avoiding the wooden spoon. It was something, at least.

For Price, the tournament was a wholly positive experience. 'It was invaluable for both parties. It's good for me because then I could see who was really engaging with the programmes. Then from their side it was really important for them to see where they are in the world rankings and what exactly they've got to learn. So to play through the tournament, get better and better each game, look at our scoring shot percentages going out, look at the way we were getting out, and then in the next game try and get better at it. Then we beat Namibia in that last game because we did all those really good things well. There were a lot of ticks throughout.'

Finally things were looking up for the US women's national team. But then Covid happened, wiping out the entire 2020 season. Price returned to Australia and was only able to see the team remotely during that whole traumatic era. When we spoke to her at the end of that year she was hopeful for the future of the national squad.

'I think they're seriously quite good. Again, I think it's just that lack of game awareness that holds them back. They haven't played as many games so they just don't know when to be able to incorporate which shots. Once we get the fitness levels up and the amount of games they are playing every year I think the gap will close really quickly. At the moment we're 31 in the world and I think we can get to 20 really quickly. Then it becomes a bit of a hard slog because we're going to be up against teams like Scotland, Netherlands and Ireland: countries that have been around for a long while that have made reasonable investment in the women's game.'

She cites the example of Thailand. 'They took ten years to go from a very low ranking and having full-time cricketers to qualify for a World Cup. We're not going to go full-time at the moment so I think it's a minimum ten years for a process to qualify for a World Cup. It doesn't mean that they're not going to be performing at a great level. They definitely could be inside the top 20 within five or six years. After that let's think about qualifying for a World Cup.'

For that to ever happen, you'd think several things would need to be put in place. A domestic structure that would involve in the first instance a higher number of competitive games between women's teams. Whilst a men's T20 Major League started in 2023, it seems an equivalent for their female counterparts is several years away at best. There would also have to be a concerted drive to increase the number of players, for which getting the sport into schools would be a prerequisite. And for that to happen, you'd need an increase in specialist coaches. None of these are going to appear overnight and they will all take money, a commodity US men's cricket has never had much of, let alone their female counterparts.

'Currently, there isn't even one regional tournament that happens between the girls,' lamented Sindhu Shriharsha in 2021. 'Building that domestic structure is the number one plan for USA Cricket. I think the girls are hungry and we are waiting for that to happen, and you will be surprised to see the talent that is going to come out of those tournaments.'

Slowly, after Covid, women's cricket started back up again in 2021. 'We've had three tiers of competition this year,' Nadia Gruny explains. 'First one is called the Intra-Regionals, so that's almost kind of like on a club level with whatever clubs can be formed in clusters in the main cities or hubs across the country. They get together and play a series of matches and then from that point teams were selected to represent the regions to play at a regional competition. Again, there are a number of matches and from there two teams were selected: one to represent the East Coast and the second team to represent the West Coast and we played in the national, championship a total of five or six games. It was fantastic.'

In Sindhu's San Francisco local progress has been made too. 'Today in the Bay Area we have enough girls to make at least two teams. We have a lot of youngsters, under-16 girls particularly. We have the Willow Cricket Academy and also the NCCA leagues which give us games so right now we're playing every weekend girls versus boys in full games.'

Lurking in the imagination of all of those involved in US women's cricket is the knowledge of what happened to soccer. At college level, the passing of the Title XI legislation in 1972, which made gender equality mandatory in education, including sporting activities, helped enormously. But the real growth came in the 1990s when the number of college women's soccer teams tripled between the USA's World Cup victories in 1991 and 1999, after which the first female professional league in the world – WUSA (Women's United Soccer Association) – was formed.

'As players we talk about it. We've all said, "Hey, see where soccer is today and where it started off,"' suggests Shriharsha. 'But you've got to understand that it took years for soccer in the US to become a mainstream sport. It took them years of what we are going through right now.'

Julie Abbott is more hopeful. 'I definitely see some parallels with soccer. I think that the women have greater opportunity to grow faster than the men's national team do. Whilst they're making tremendous progress and things are looking bright on the men's side of things, I think that they have got a harder pathway. With the women it's more of a blank canvas. We have an opportunity to move women's cricket in the USA more expediently and go on to give greater support just like the women's soccer programmes have over here.'

If enterprising school boards could find a way of getting cricket on to the curriculum then there's no reason why this can't happen. Soccer, after all, was sold to schoolgirls and college kids as a wholesome alternative to macho US sports like American football so you can easily envisage cricket, with its emphasis on etiquette and fair play, being offered up as a similar contrast to baseball. Whatever happens, after decades and decades of struggle, the trajectory of the women's game in the US is now only heading one way: upwards.

8

If you build it, will they come?

Two Southern cricket stadiums

ONE MAY forcibly argue that the American 21st century began in earnest on the night of 7 November 2000, as deeply polarising events surrounding the 2000 United States presidential election began to unfold. Central to the prolonged drama was the state of Florida, whose 25 electoral votes would ultimately determine the outcome of an incredibly tight race between Democratic candidate Al Gore and Republican candidate George W. Bush junior, the latter being the scion of former president George W. Bush senior.

As election night unfolded, initial media projections declared Florida for Gore, then shifted to Bush, and finally labelled the state as too close to call. With a razor-thin margin separating the candidates, the nation's attention turned to Florida, where the hitherto nondescript and unknown Broward County quickly became emblematic of the Sunshine State's broader electoral chaos.

The focal point of the controversy lay in the interpretation of voter intent as recorded by the infamous punch-card voting system. Voters were required to punch holes next to their candidate of choice, but this antiquated method led to widespread issues. Many ballots featured 'hanging chads' – partially punched holes that machines struggled to read – as well as 'dimpled chads', where voters had attempted to vote but failed to fully puncture the card. The result was thousands of ballots with ambiguous markings, leaving officials and legal teams grappling with the question of voter intent.

Electoral officials were left with the unenviable and gruelling task of meticulously performing manual recounts under the full glare of a media eager to capture the controversy as it unfolded in real time. The spectacle of election officials holding ballots up to the light, squinting to assess whether a dimpled chad indicated a vote, became a defining image. The sincere anguish of disenfranchised voters became the defining emotion as the American democratic process was tested to its limits.

A distinct lack of uniform standards for evaluating disputed ballots added fuel to the fire. Each county in Florida applied different criteria, and within Broward

County individual election officials often interpreted ballots differently. A lack of consistency thus fuelled accusations of partisanship, with Republicans alleging that Democratic-leaning counties like Broward were bending the rules to favour Gore. The counter-argument was that the accusations were false and simply an extension of a civil rights struggle with its roots going back to the founding of the nation itself.

The legal battle over the Florida recount escalated rapidly, culminating in a series of court rulings. The Florida Supreme Court ordered a statewide manual recount, but the US Supreme Court dramatically and decisively intervened. Citing the 14th amendment, it issued a controversial 5-4 decision in Bush v. Gore on 12 December 2000, effectively halting the recount. With the recount stopped, Bush was declared the winner in Florida by a margin of just 537 votes, thus securing the presidency.

The aftermath of the 2000 election, once the media had returned to the safety of their studios and editorial offices, left a lasting impact upon American electoral processes. Perhaps it was this intense collective experience that in due course led to Broward County's electoral officials, in close conjunction with the electorate, to embark upon a process that would ultimately lead to the building of the first purpose-built cricket stadium in the US.

* * *

But before we relate the details of that stadium let's set the scene. From Washington DC to Broward County by car requires little if any navigation; one simply swings on to the Interstate-95 (I-95) and drives some 1,030 miles. Journeying south upon the I-95 is an odyssey in and of itself. It is one of the oldest routes of the Interstate Highway System and skirts the entire eastern seaboard. From Washington DC the I-95 snakes through the states of Virginia, North Carolina, South Carolina and Georgia before hitting Florida.

En route, even from the front seat of a speeding car, the ghosts of the past make their presence felt. It begins as soon as one crosses the beautiful Potomac River, the name of which is an echo of the indigenous presence that whilst no longer culturally dominant still finds its representation in the place names and landscapes that the I-95 passes through.

Heading into Virginia the ghosts of colonial history are everywhere. At frequent intervals, signs invite the curious tourist to visit one or other of the numerous battlefields upon which the American Civil War was fought. Fredericksburg, Richmond, Williamsburg, Yorktown ... Anglicised names of towns upon the front lines of a political, cultural and military conflict that led to over a million deaths. A conflict that has is been covered elsewhere in this book led to the birth of baseball and the demise of cricket in the late 19th century.

Continuing through the Carolinas, North and South, the landscape unfurls in broad, lazy sweeps. From Roanoke Rapids, the I-95 skirts first Raleigh and then the US army town of Fayetteville. The Marquis de La Fayette is the source of Fayetteville's French origins. As a French nobleman and military officer, he gained invaluable experience as a member of George Washington's Continental Army during the American Revolutionary War. He subsequently put this experience to good use during the French Revolution.

Augmenting the invitations to visit old battlefields, the I-95 traveller passing through the Carolinas will receive invitations to inspect the remnants of slave plantations such as Historic Stagville. Such plantations were the final destination for millions of West African men, women and children. Stagville is a 165-acre State Historic Site, a visit to which yields keen insights into the juxtapositions of bondage and wealth, injustice and resistance, slavery and freedom.

Continuing further, or shall we say deeper, south, the highway acquires a sort of hypnotic rhythm. The names of towns flick past in a lazy procession – Turbeville, Alcolu, Walterboro – places that travellers only become acquainted with during brief pit-stops leading to another gas station receipt. The hypnotic spell is momentarily broken as the

I-95 crosses Lake Marion, passes by the National Golf Club of Santee, and makes a straight beeline across the Savannah River into the state of Georgia.

Despite being the 13th (and final) American colony, the city of Savannah had the good fortune to have been established without the need of resorting to arms. This was due to the cordial relations between Tomochichi, the local indigenous chief, and General James Oglethorpe. Unhindered by distractions, Oglethorpe laid the city out in a series of grids, whereby wide-open streets are intertwined with shady public squares and parks. Its beauty was such that the Union General Sherman, on his famous 'March to the Sea' during the American Civil War, offered the city to Abraham Lincoln as a Christmas gift rather than destroy it.

Back on the I-95, Georgia passes sleepily by. The landscape is distinctly flat with and marshes spreading out on either side of the road. Rivers, creeks, bluffs, sounds, inlets and islands act as natural buffers between the highway and the Atlantic. The air takes on a faint tang of salt and the road presses on, dragging you ever southward until, at last, you cross the St. Marys River and pass under the great sign that declares: Welcome to Florida.

Passing through Jacksonville, the northern stretches of Florida along I-95 are still somewhat tame – palms begin to mix with the pines and the exits promise fresh oranges and boiled peanuts in equal measure. But the billboards – oh, the billboards! They no longer try to sell you on pecans and peaches. Now they are hawking the grand and the bizarre: alligator wrestling, mermaid shows, discount Disney tickets, and lawyers who appear to be engaged in a blood feud with one another.

Pressing further south the trees thin out, the land grows even flatter, and the very sky seems wider, as if Florida itself is trying to stretch out under all that sun. You start to notice that everything is just a little … stranger. Gas stations sell fried gator tails alongside fountain drinks, and small-town souvenir shops have a suspiciously large number of signs warning against feeding the wildlife.

Inland it is all lakes and nature reserves, water is everywhere, and the wildlife is distinctly aquatic. In the ever-present heat the local roads shimmer and appear to hover just above the waterline. The humidity is perpetually high, as are many of the inhabitants it would seem, but they are probably simply adapting to the conditions. Because the reality is that in Florida there really is no point in rushing anything. Indeed, to rush is simply to invite an ocean of sweat and a whole host of bother.

Every I-95 exit now seems to lead to a beach with an Anglicised name – Beverly Beach, Butler Beach, Flagler

Beach, etc. However, exploring the history of Daytona Beach reveals that it was once inhabited by the Timucua people. Further research uncovers that the Second 'Seminole' War, aka the Florida War, lasted from 1835 to 1842, and was fought between the government of the United States and groups of indigenous people collectively known as Seminoles.

The war was triggered by attempts to impose a treaty of tribal resettlement from the area now known as the Florida Panhandle. Today several reservations scattered across mostly southern Florida allow the communities to continue practising their way of life, as embodied by the Green Corn Ceremony. Over time they have adapted to the new circumstances and are financially savvy to the extent that amongst other investments in their collective portfolio is the Hard Rock Cafe chain!

Passing by the great sprawl of Orlando seems to trigger something different; Miami is fast approaching and back on the I-95 a sign indicates the proximity of Cape Canaveral. When the weather is good and NASA is in the mood, you may stop and gaze upwards at the next glorious chapter in modern America's race to space, and then probably return to your cruise ship docked conveniently nearby.

Whilst the Kennedy Space Center is where the action mostly happens nowadays, pretty much the entire Cape has been used for aeronautical and missile research since the 1940s. From the Apollo missions of the 1960s, via the Skylab mission of the early 1970s, to the Space Shuttle missions of the 1980s and into the 20th century, Cape Canaveral has played a huge role in the project of US power. It continues today with the activities of SpaceX, the Elon Musk-owned entity that at the time of writing frequently launches its Falcon 9 series of rockets from launch pads upon the Cape.

Before hitting the environs of Miami, the I-95 takes you past one other place of particular note, namely West Palm Beach. The world's epicentre of uncool cool, the people here seem to move in two distinct modes: the serenity of folks who have never known the discomfort of a bank account lacking in commas; and the fraughtness of those who scurry and toil to ensure the first group never has to lift so much as a finger.

It is of course the home from home of the man who has become 45th and 47th President of the United States, one Donald J. Trump. Mar-a-Lago, his primary residence, is both a resort and a National Historic Landmark. According to the National Historic Landmarks programme: 'This sprawling, Mediterranean-style villa, exemplifies the baronial way of life of the wealthy.' Membership of the Mar-a-Lago Club costs an initial $200,000, after which a yearly $14,000 secures access to the highest levels of US power.

Golf is, of course, on the menu and fortunately the Trump International Golf Club is but a buggy ride away.

So as one may have observed by now, we began in one place of power, namely Washington DC, to that of another place of power, Mar-a-Lago. Only Miami awaits before the Everglades stretch out to the endless vistas of the Florida Keys. The journey south has been long, humid and hot, but the I-95 has done its job and brought us to Broward County, where the chads once hung.

Broward County, Florida started out in the 1950s as a predominantly white, suburban retirement haven. Its origins trace back to developer Herbert Sadkin, who envisioned a planned suburban community catering to predominantly white middle-class families and retirees. Comprising of some 31 cities, it has evolved over time to become one of the most ethnically diverse counties in the entire United States. Due to an abundance of job opportunities, Broward has become a thriving centre of Caribbean culture with a growing Latino population. Once a swing county, it is now a firmly Democratic stronghold.

The pulsing heartbeat of the county is the City of Lauderhill, winner of the 2005 'All America City' award. Incorporated in 1959, Lauderhill began as a series of off-the-shelf housing developments augmented by various public buildings, including of course sports facilities. Gradually, due to the demographic shift, Lauderhill has come to be affectionately referred to as 'Little Jamaica'. The Caribbean influence is evident everywhere from the rhythmic sounds of reggae and soca drifting from neighbourhood shops to the annual events like the Caribbean Carnival that attract thousands. Many local radio stations and businesses cater specifically to Caribbean communities, making the city a cultural hub for South Florida's West Indian diaspora.

Back in the distant days of November 2004, we had come all this way simply to explore the persistent rumours of a new cricket stadium. It was being implied that a stadium was being built by the community for the community – a refreshingly bottom-up form of power, a juxtaposition if you will to the excesses of Mar-a-Lago. A visit to the mayoral office at Lauderhill City Hall was mentioned as being the key to proving the veracity or otherwise of the whisperings.

From our base in languid Coral Gables, we once again swung on to the I-95 and for once we headed north rather than south. We were en route to interview the folks who seemed to be in the know. Leaving the I-95 at Junction 29B, we head on the 838 West towards Lauderhill City Hall. Our somewhat singular intent was to go straight to the horse's mouth and speak with the mayor in person, i.e. unfiltered access.

But it's not always so easy getting access to an important and busy person. Schedules need to be considered, background checks to be made, questions to be asked, integrity to be verified. And so it was that our initial interview was with the operations officer of Lauderhill City Hall, an Italian-American woman called Leslie Tropepe. As we entered her office it became quite apparent that we were talking with the type of down-to-earth, no-nonsense public servant that makes a difference.

Until the turn of the century her exposure to cricket was net zero, so what led her we wondered to now being part of a team helping to oversee the construction of the first purpose-built cricket stadium in the US?

'In the November 7, 2000 election, the same election that led to all the fuss and bother at the national level, the county of Broward decided to put to the electorate a referendum upon whether or not to raise a $400 million parks and green spaces public bond. That is to say, the public had the opportunity to either vote for or against raising a loan to the tune of $400 million in order to improve the parks and free spaces throughout the county. Once the votes had been tallied it was quite clear that they had voted a resounding yes.

'Following the announcement of the public bond issuance, a big piece of land that used to be an AT&T antennae farm came up for sale. This property was on our industrial park area, a depressed area on a main thoroughfare in the city. The county officials were keen to purchase it, but we at City Hall were somewhat hesitant, however in the end after consultation with local citizens the land purchase went through. Building upon this, the city decided to invest millions of dollars so as to purchase two very large pieces of property next to the park. The end result was that both the county and the city ended up owning large and adjacent chunks of land, thereby meaning that collectively we could control our own destiny as far as the proposed park was concerned.

'Once the land purchases were confirmed, the next step was to initiate community conversations in respect of to what activities the park would support. During the initial set of conversations, in meeting after meeting, people came out of the woodwork to state their preferred activity was cricket. I'd never seen them before but they only ever said one word, and that word was cricket!'

Against this backdrop of a public bond being issued at the county level, further funds being committed at the city level, land purchases being signed, and strong community support for cricket, momentum for building a cricket stadium became inexorable. However, none of the City Hall's team had any experience of building a cricket stadium. Furthermore, the county took quite some persuading that some of the precious bond money ought to be allocated towards a potentially risky project.

Leslie continues the story: 'We had to work with the county and say to them, "Hey county, we've really been investigating this and it is potentially a big deal." Yes, they will need cricket fields for their Sunday leagues and weekday night cricket, but we also need something that can host international cricket. We had to explain to the county folks that these guys are cricket thirsty, they're watching it on the internet, they're streaming it from pay per view, they're going to certain clubs that have it on the TV 24/7, in the middle of the night simply to watch the cricket.

'You have to realise that it was a completely American group of people making the decisions. We said to the county folks, "Just look at the number of people here from cricket-playing countries." We were already celebrating various Caribbean-island independence days and hosting numerous Caribbean cultural events. There was still a lot of education to do, but a research trip to Trinidad proved a big help as it revealed the potential international dimension, particularly the idea of bringing the World Cup to the city in some capacity. So it wasn't too long before they had all caught on, and then even the mayor began to play!'

When even the mayor has caught the cricketing bug, you know that something big is going to happen. A few hours after interviewing Leslie, we are sat face to face with Richard Kaplan, elected mayor of Lauderhill City. He is tall, avuncular, a born conversationalist, and smart without any airs or graces. As with Leslie we immediately take to him. Straight off the bat he outlines where he feels the project should be heading towards.

'I'm anticipating that Lauderhill becomes the cricket capital of the United States.' Impressive ambition, we think to ourselves. Mayor Kaplan continued: 'First of all several development efforts are coming to the City of Lauderhill that converge on improving the parks and recreational spaces. There have been cricket programmes around the city but hitherto City Hall wasn't particularly involved – now it is acting as a focal point. Secondly, we are exploring a sister cities programme to act as an engine of business and cultural exchange; specifically we are looking at Chaguanas in Trinidad and Tobago.

'We visited Chaguanas and noted the importance of cricket and that's when the World Cup was suggested to us. They said that it was coming to the Caribbean in 2007 and enquired whether the US would be interested in bidding for the World Cup. I said, "Well, we're not part of the Caribbean." And they were like, "No, the US can bid on it." And so began the concept of bidding on the World Cup.

'So now you have this whole cricket environment being created. A 25-mile stretch of road along the US-441 passes through 14 cities and two or three Indian reservations and has been earmarked by the county for massive improvements. The City of Lauderhill owns a slice and that was designated as the site of a new regional park, which is where a cricket stadium capable of hosting World Cup games is to be built, along with other facilities of course. It's all coming together with completion projected to be September 2006.'

And thus was a dream made a reality, not by the usual machinations of plotting, scheming, wheeling and dealing, but by listening, by coordinating, by executing upon a local and regional plan with no agenda other than to make something happen. In many ways it helped that none of the local officials involved had any real connection to cricket, i.e. they had no skin in the game other than to serve their communities.

Earl Hall, attorney for the City of Lauderhill, expands on this essential point. 'Lauderhill is ground zero for cricket. In that capacity I have had the privilege of helping to develop all the construction plans as well as being involved with the World Cup bid. Normally there are layers of politics that get in the way of a project such as this, particularly with the sports franchise model in which wealthy owners typically drive the project. However, in this case there is no personalised agenda – it is simply the right thing to do. This project is 100% owned by the people.'

And thus, via democratically mandated state grants, county funds and city contributions, the $70 million of finance was pooled together to allow construction to commence in 2005. With seasonal hurricanes sufficiently violent to merit Lauderhill's designation as a high-velocity hurricane zone, by necessity all buildings need to be designed with wind-resistant capabilities, with concrete exoskeletons able to sustain winds above 140mph. Such considerations would of course make their way into the construction of a special purpose cricket stadium.

However, by far the most important aspect of building a cricket venue aspiring to ICC certification is of course the pitch, particularly the hallowed square. In the absence of local expertise, sages were summoned from distant lands so as to make delicate horticultural assessments.

Eventually on 9 November 2007 the first and still to this day only ICC-certified purpose-built cricket stadium in the United States came into existence. The inaugural cricket tournament was the Martin Luther King T20 held in January 2008, appropriately enough it featured local players. In May 2008; the first international tournament was held, drawing teams from Canada, Pakistan and the West Indies. Finally real history was made on 22 May 2010, when the first full international cricket match on American soil was held between New Zealand and Sri Lanka.

But as we have seen there were criticisms of the pitch and the facilities. USACA's deal with New Zealand Cricket in 2010 to create Cricket Holdings America was supposed to entice the Test-playing nations to come to Florida, as well as a T20 league. These did not transpire, and criticism of the stadium began to grow.

As early as August 2009 the *South Florida Sun Sentinel* had detailed the criticisms from the local community in an article bitingly entitled: 'Broward Built It, But Cricket Hasn't Come'. Two years later an editorial in the paper described the stadium as 'a legendary example of Broward officials setting taxpayer money on fire'.

Then-USACA CEO Don Lockerbie put a brave face on it: 'We understand that there will be commentary and a lot of frustration by the stakeholders who feel that the stadium hasn't seen its fair share of international cricket,' Lockerbie told the paper. 'The point is, the United States itself has not been the powerhouse of cricket.'

Whilst the reluctance of the ICC full members to play at Broward County can be partly explained by US cricket's appalling governance, a more serious mark against it has been the lack of support from the local Floridian community.

This was never better demonstrated than during 2016 and 2018 when the Caribbean Premier League staged some games at Broward County, as US cricket writer Peter Della Penna remembers.

'The ticket data overwhelmingly showed that all the credit card zip codes billing addresses were from New York, San Francisco, Dallas, Detroit, Chicago. Everybody who was going to Florida had to fly in Friday night and fly out on Sunday night or Monday morning. Nobody in Florida was buying tickets to those games.

'I distinctly remember in 2018 going to Liberty Avenue in Queens and at the subway stop there was a huge CPL advertising banner hanging over the NY city subway stop and it was to advertise games in Florida. And the CPL paid for that ad because they knew the majority of their ticket buyers for matches in Florida were from the Guyanese community in New York or the Trinidadian community.'

Della Penna's assessment is blunt. 'Nobody wants to go there. They don't have any hometown loyalty. They never had any loyalty. If anybody has gone to any games in Lauderhill, the data shows if you schedule a game on a weekday nobody shows up.'

Inevitably this meant it couldn't be kept as merely a cricket facility and indeed since 2013 soccer, rugby and

Australian Rules football have all been played in the stadium.

Finally in 2019, Broward County saw a USA team make its ODI debut at the stadium. They beat Papua New Guinea, but in a rain-soaked match USA prevailed only by the Duckworth–Lewis method and it hardly represented a glorious new chapter for the troubled stadium.

Post-Covid the stadium was passed over as a venue for Major League Cricket in favour of Grand Prairie in Dallas. But it has belatedly claimed a space on the world stage. Back in 2004 Mayor Kaplan had expressed his hope that, 'Someday we'll be able to actually have a World Cup in the United States.' Two decades later in 2024 his hope was fulfilled when the group stages of the Men's T20 World Cup were held in the US. On 16 June, after three previous matches had been cancelled due to rain, Pakistan beat Ireland by three wickets at the Broward Stadium.

The stadium's legacy will endure as a cornerstone of cricket's development in America. It came about because of public servants seeing an opportunity. Let's leave the last words to Mayor Kaplan, who after 30 years of public service in the City of Lauderhill, finally retired in November 2018: 'If you want the United States to get more involved with cricket then you're going to have more native-born Americans getting involved – it can be done.'

* * *

Twenty years later and 678 miles to the north of Broward, we stand in Morrisville, North Carolina. Morrisville is a suburb of the city of Raleigh and whilst Raleigh has a current population of just under half a million it doesn't compare to other US megalopolises. It's not even the biggest city in North Carolina (that title belongs to Charlotte). And yet Morrisville is a cricketing centre as important as New York, Los Angeles or Texas. In some ways, more so.

It's a Saturday evening in September and we're here at its mecca: Church Street Park. A Minor League game featuring the local side the Morrisville Raptors should be in full swing, but for reasons we'll come to, it's been cancelled. So local cricketing devotee, writer and commentator Nate Hays should be enjoying an evening off. Instead, he's talking to us. 'It's a special place. It's not like …' He pauses. 'The rest of the country has got a lot more challenges than Morrisville does.'

He describes the scene that should have greeted us here, that you'd see when Minor or Major League games are played here: 'First of all we'll have maybe a couple of hundred people before the sun goes down. Once the second innings comes there will be maybe 1,000 people in there on a Saturday night. And it'll be kids, a lot of families with kids. It'll be the cricketers who have finished their games,

who want a place to sit around with their friends and …
hide their alcohol. They usually have it in a paper cup.

'It's so fun. We have regulars who come out to watch
the whole game and set up a chair and a lot of times it's
expats from England or New Zealand or South Africa.
They love it! They all come out and say, "This reminds me
of back home."'

As we talk we can see South Asian families milling
about, some kids playing and on the other side people
playing on the tennis courts that are part of the facility.
'People are utilising the park on a daily basis,' says Nate.
'To go for a walk. It's a part of their community. It's a place
that people like to meet anyway.'

Over the next few days we'll hear a lot of that word
'community'. Ultimately it explains how Church Street Park
came to be built. But first of all a community had to develop
and the reason for that is the Research Triangle. Set up in
1959, the Research Triangle Park is the largest science or
business park in the US.

It's always attracted talent from all over the world, but
around the turn of the millennium it seems the number
of South Asians in the locale began to reach critical mass.
'Research Triangle Park brought a lot of South Asians here
gradually and then of course they want to do something
with their time,' says Hays. 'They would find public grounds

and talk to their municipal parks and rec and have wickets put in and pay for that.'

Gradually teams began to be formed and in 2009 the Triangle League started. The following day we head back to Church Street Park where we meet its production manager and former president, Babar Baig, a softly-spoken fellow who moved to the local area back in 2000 and has thus seen the huge explosion of interest in the quarter century since.

'When I moved here there was no cricket – not playing. The only thing there was concrete cricket where you go to a parking lot and play with a tape ball. We did that a lot. There weren't a lot of local players so my cousin, who was also a cricket fanatic, would have to go out of town to bring them in.'

A few of these new teams entered the existing local Carolina Cricket League. 'The issue with that league was that there was a lot of travel involved, so we'd be driving out of town for an hour or an hour and a half to play cricket and then two clubs decided, "Hey, why can't we have our own league here?"'

Initially the TCL, as it's commonly known around here, comprised of 'just eight or nine teams' playing 35-over games. Thirteen years later Baig estimates that there are 64 in the Premier League with 48 in the T20 league and an incredible 160 in the tennis ball league. 'And there's a waiting list,' he adds. 'It's first come, first served. You just send an email today and you've got to wait until you get your time. Sometimes it can take three years before you get in.'

As the tech sector expanded as the 21st century progressed, more and more South Asians came over to Morrisville and the Research Triangle for work and found a ready-made community. And they began playing cricket. Nothing unusual about it really. But in Morrisville, cricket had a crucial convert in the town's mayor.

We meet Mark Stohlman the following day. He's 64, though he could easily pass for ten years younger, and he's still playing cricket. He had enjoyed a successful life in business. Then in 2007 he joined the town council. 'I joined as one of the concerned citizens. You know, "Make a difference in the town" and so on. In 2013 I became the mayor, and I had one term that ended in 2017.

'About a third of the residents here are South Asian so I kind of immersed myself into the culture quite a bit. And with that came doing man of the match and coin-tossing before cricket matches. I didn't know the game. I'd just show up and hand out a trophy and that was pretty much it.

'So I began to become familiar with the game. My son would play in the local rec league – at that time he was 12 or 13 years old. We noticed that Morrisville started letting local cricket leagues use their softball fields and then set up pitches and things like that. But if you were a really serious baseball player, you'd opt for Raleigh or West Cary or one of the larger municipalities, you didn't necessarily do that in Morrisville. Morrisville kind of flipped.'

Then in 2012 the local municipality bought the land at Church Street. The original idea was to use it as a baseball complex with enough space for four fields. 'It would be what they call a pinwheel park,' says Stohlman. 'If you can imagine a home base being close to each other and a quarter of the pie kind of radiating out so the four fields are in a pinwheel.'

But it soon became clear that creating four baseball fields would be very expensive. 'There's a lot of stone, rock and clay here and to do a proper field you need irrigation. I don't know if they're as finicky as cricket, but baseball fields certainly need a lot of work, especially four of them. The cost was simply going to be too high, so they opted to just make it a big round multi-use field.

'I won't take the credit for it, but someone said, "Well that looks like a cricket field, do you mind if we make it a cricket pitch?" and we let them do it. We have a big following here. Maybe we can get bigger matches and stuff like that and then there was the real key to this whole thing.'

The key individual was a West Indies legend who had been coaching in the local area for some time. Alvin Kallicharran was reluctant to speak to us about his role in creating Church Street Park but by all accounts, it was pivotal. 'I would meet him at various functions,' says Stohlman. 'And by 2015 there was this kind of turning point – we thought we had a pitch, but we didn't know what we were doing so he invited the ICC out to show up here in 2015.

'We had a big meeting out on the pitch. We practised batting and bowling and they said, "This has the makings of a really nice ground but this pitch is junk. I mean it's absolute trash." And it was.'

By 2015 USACA were suspended once more from the ICC and it was looking likely that their final expulsion was just a matter of time. The ICC were looking ahead and already taking a more hands-on role regarding the errant child of the associates. Giving encouragement to an initiative like Church Street Park was merely preparing the way for what (in theory) could be a flourishing of the game in the 2020s.

Stohlman added: 'They really liked what they saw here. They came to town hall and we made a presentation. We had a good relationship with the ICC, and they said if you can get this pitch in order in the next couple of years, we can get you some international matches.

'Nothing much happened for a couple of years and in 2018, they said, "Okay, if you can get this pitch ready, we can give you the World Cup qualifiers here." And we had less than six months or so to get this pitch in order. They said they'd give us Dave Agnew, an Australian who was in New Zealand at the time. "He will come and help you get this thing dialled in." We didn't know the first thing about pitches or anything else. The main thing is that we had to dig out the entire box.'

An entirely new pitch had to be constructed, which involved bringing in some 2,500 bags of clay in from the Midwest. 'It was a huge mess getting this thing ready,' remembers Stohlman. 'We had 2,500 bags sitting out there on pallets. And people were washing. There was turf on the top and it had to be washed because you couldn't have the foreign soil attached to it.'

Under Agnew's guidance, somehow the pitch was ready for the Americas T20 World Cup qualifiers, which saw the US take on Belize, Panama and old rivals Canada. Perhaps unwisely the ICC had scheduled the games in September, which is hurricane season, and Mother Nature duly did her worst. Just days before the first game Hurricane Florence hit Morrisville.

'We had 20 inches of rain here,' remembers Stohlman. 'So you can imagine what it did to this field.' But the cricket community rose to the challenge. So determined were local people to see international cricket go ahead in Morrisville that a small army of volunteers turned up to drain the pitch. 'This is before we had super-soppers or anything – we were out there with towels and buckets and everything else, just hauling the water off.'

Incredibly, the pitch was ready in time and the community enjoyed an unforgettable week of cricket. As expected, the group came down to the two games between the US and Canada. The first went down to a super over which Canada nudged by two runs. However, three days later the USA exacted revenge in another incredible game. At 65/6 they seemed dead and buried, but somehow Steven Taylor, playing one of the greatest innings by any US player, hauled his team back from the brink. He secured the win with a six from the final ball.

There was a full-scale pitch invasion. Pandemonium. Scenes never before witnessed in US cricket. 'That was the night when it changed,' says Nate Hays. 'The local community had ensured the games went ahead. We had turned up – 3,000 of us for the Canada game. And the USA had delivered. It was the first time lots of people truly felt proud of a US team.'

Aaman Patel remembers it well. A youth player turned commentator, he was just 15 at the time, and like many cricket-crazy youngsters was volunteering that night. 'For a lot of us young kids it was the first time we saw the USA team play in person, play live and so just presented this like, "Oh wow really cool, there is a US team. This is a real thing."'

He remembers the final-ball drama as 'pure frenzy. Steven Taylor hits the six. He throws his bat in the air. He's running around with his helmet. The entire team rushes the field. Everyone rushed the field at the end. Everyone was in a frenzy, because obviously USA won but it was just a real moment where the whole community wrapped its hands around the team.'

Aaman moved to Morrisville with his parents, aged six, in 2009. He has grown up watching this incredible story gradually unfold. Indeed, his parents bought a house deliberately close to the then-only cricket field in Morrisville, at Shilol. 'My dad convinced my mom to buy a house here so he could just walk to the practice field for a game. At the time that was the only place they were playing cricket. So to see it from that stage to now is pretty cool, and there's grounds out at Fuquay and Chapel Hill as well as Church Street Park.'

Speaking to him the following day, you can sense the pride he feels when he describes Minor League coming to Morrisville in 2021, followed by Major League in 2023.

Aaman remembers commentating at the first few rounds at Grand Prairie in Texas before it switched to Church Street Park. 'I was like, "I don't know how Church Street is going to compete with Grand Prairie."

'Come back to Church Street, they made it so nice. They got advertising around the rim. The stadium seating had come in. It was a really cool thing. I was really impressed with it and I thought the players loved it too. Every time we asked them about it at the press conferences they seemed pretty pleased.

'I mean Morrisville is not known for anything. Nothing much happens here. There's Raleigh in one direction, Durham in another. But we have our own cricket bundle and for that to be shown on an international stage I think surprised a lot of folks.'

And yet despite the cricket-crazy ready-made audience there is in Morrisville, despite its growing reputation for being a darn nice place to play the game, Church Street Park does have its issues. Drainage is one – the very fact there are no Minor League games here this weekend is testament to that. The floodlights need improving too, and both of these issues will need investment.

The funding for Church Street has come from a variety of sources including local taxation and American Cricket Enterprises for the stands. Major League spent nearly $2 million on bleachers and practice facilities at Church Street. We ask Mark Stohlman whether the further necessary improvements might be covered by a bond, similar to that which funded Broward County.

'Well, bonds require citizens to vote for them and you'd better have a pretty good story,' he smiles. 'If you said, "Ten million dollars is going to be for cricket," you might get some local opposition. It's mainly for affordable housing or setting up transit stops. They're for particular purposes. I'd like to think that you could do a bond for cricket but the reality is you have to sell them because it means a tax increase.'

Stohlman left the mayoralty in 2017, but local government remains supportive of the cricketing community here. Certainly Babar Baig seems appreciative of everything they do. 'Morrisville is like beyond … I don't have words,' he says. 'They are so supportive. You name it, the whole town will be here. The council men will be here. The mayor will be there. Town officials, town managers – they all want to know what's happening, what can they do, how they can fix it.'

Baig often has to field calls from other leagues around the US asking for advice. 'You don't see this kind of support in other towns, unfortunately. I've been talking with people in Atlanta and Washington DC for almost three years now. They are very dedicated people but unfortunately, they do not have support from their local town.'

But whilst Church Street Park has a community and its local government behind it, as well as Major League, it seems to have been ignored by the new national body. Since those joyous scenes of September 2018, not one USA game has been played at Church Street Park, much to the chagrin of the locals.

'They have purposely not scheduled games at Morrisville,' claims Nate Hays. 'Because they know they'll get 2,000 people out easily and if they advertise they'll get 3,000. And they hate it. They hate the fact that they would have to organise it and they would have to spend the money. It would be a massive hassle for them. If you're going to have a game there and you want to sell tickets you've got to put in a temporary fence.

'If you don't want to charge tickets you still have to pay for the police to usher fans in and out and you still have to pay for parking offsite or have a shuttle going to and from, which is fine. It's not an astronomical price. But USA Cricket are very cheap and they don't get a lot of money from sponsors – they simply don't have the money to manage a crowd.'

Indeed, the governing body elected to stage the warm-up games for the T20 World Cup at the Prairie View complex in Houston. But Prairie View can barely be called a ground – it does not even have changing rooms or toilets for the players, let alone any spectators who might turn up to support their national team.

To Hays' mind, it's a short-sighted approach. 'Wouldn't you want your team to be playing in front of a crowd all the time? It'll grow the game and raise its profile, just because of the appearance. And the broadcasts … it helps so much because if it looks like people are there – and we can make that happen easily with a good broadcast – then guess what? You do get more sponsors, or at least it would be easier to attract them.'

And whilst it hosts Major League games, it seems unlikely the organisers would ever create a new franchise here. 'Morrisville is not in the queue to expand, unfortunately,' predicts Hays. 'I wish Major League Cricket had taken the approach and said, "We're going to build our brand in the communities that really want us to be there and are going to show up to the game." That's the way you spread the game. You popularise the game. Some of the biggest communities in the country for soccer like Nebraska are like that.'

He explains that in the US, very often it's the teams based in smaller communities that have the most fervent and committed fans. 'You'll see a lot of sports teams in large cities when if the team isn't doing well for a long period of time the stands get empty. Miami is a big city.

But if the Marlins have been bad for a couple of years in baseball the stadium is empty. It's because the city has a lot of competition for your time and attention.

'Whereas in Morrisville the cricket fans tend to like that their small town is such a big hub of cricket in the US. It's a source of pride. And so they're happy to come out whenever anything is happening and they're happy to be involved in it. Because there's not a ton of things that are happening in Morrisville all the time.'

But it is undoubtedly a nice place to live. Everywhere is within a short distance – a ten-minute drive tops. A community has grown up here, with Church Street Park at its centre. It's meant that things have happened fast in Morrisville, faster than anywhere else in the country with a South Asian population of comparable size. It's also given the cricket here its own unique character.

'It's going to sound bad,' Hays warns us, 'but cricket here in North Carolina … it's kind of like a suburban version of cricket. It's upper-middle-class families. That's how I would describe it. And young adults who want to keep playing the game. Whereas in Florida you have a mix of Caribbeans, and you have that mix of suburban expats, upper-middle class. New York and a lot of people from all over the world. It's not as class homogenous in those areas. It's pretty class homogenous here, unfortunately.'

'It's so easy here,' confirms Babar Baig. 'I can walk here, to be honest with you. This whole town has so many streets and walkways – it's so accessible for people to come to this field. You don't need to worry about how long to drive.

'And that's the key point for us. Any potential ground for the league has to be 30 minutes max and if it's over 30 minutes we say sorry we can't. We don't want to go out of our reach. If we go out of reach, then it's pointless. Because we remember how we started. We don't want to drive too far. We want to stay close to where we are, stay close to our house. There are so many Indian restaurants here and so many grocery stores also. It's a perfect place to live and that's why it's just wonderful.'

Unlike the larger cities, there seems to be little rivalry between the various ethnic groups that make up the cricket nation. Whilst New York's league system is divided between Caribbean, Indian, Pakistani and so on, here the smaller geographical space means that everybody has to rub along. Baig says: 'Instead of having multiple groups we work together. Everybody wants to play cricket, why can't we work together? And you don't see that everywhere.

'I was a president of a league where Pakistani players were just 1% of the league and a lot of people were shocked how that is possible. But it's the work that you do, right? It's the community. I have never thought that they think, "You're a

Pakistani." We're here to play cricket, right? It's a mindset for everybody. If you live in that environment, you become that environment, right? And we built that environment for a very long time and that's why it's very sustainable.'

Is there an air of smug small-town satisfaction to this? Perhaps. But as a blueprint for growing the game successfully in the US Morrisville has few rivals. Baig estimates that there are '200 to 300' kids now playing in the Triangle League. 'Every year we produce two or three who are playing in the Minor League and they are picked for the national team as well.'

For the first time it seems there is a clear pathway for young players. Aaman Patel rattles off a list of Triangle League youngsters who have graduated to play for the USA – Utkarsh Srivastava, Sanjay Stanley, Abhiram Bolisetty, Rohan Phadke and the leg-spinner Aditya Gupta. 'We have probably some of the better middle-order batters here,' he says. 'I think our guys tend to have an ability to play a little bit quicker.'

Morrisville may be reaching the limit of its possibility. There's little prospect of a Major League franchise coming here, and without investment in the pitch, Church Street Park will surely be overtaken by other venues for cricket in the US. But it is an example of what's possible, with supportive local government, good organisation, a growing pool of players and a nurturing environment.

9

Into the Heartlands

*Can cricket find a place in the US
sporting mainstream?*

NO MATTER what the current president and his MAGA movement might think, America is and always has been a nation of migrants. Its history, culture, politics and indeed its sport have all been shaped by the changing patterns of immigration over time. But perhaps more than any sport, US cricket's history has been shaped by incomers. Indeed, without them it wouldn't have survived.

As we have seen, new arrivals from the Caribbean kept the game alive in cities like New York after World War One and it has been another wave of migration that has taken US cricket forward in the last 50 to 60 years, this time from South Asia.

In 2023 there are 6.5 million South Asian Americans, or 1.95% of the total US population. This makes them the second-largest migrant group in the country, second only to Mexican Americans. You'd be forgiven for being surprised at this figure, given how inconspicuous the Indian diaspora in the US has been up until recently. Notoriously, for years the only South Asian American cultural figure that had any sort of recognition was Apu, the cartoon owner of the Kwik-E-Mart on *The Simpsons*. (This and the general dearth of South Asian representation within US culture was itself explored by Hari Kondabolu in his 2017 documentary *The Problem With Apu*.) This is changing however, not least in the realm of national politics – the 2024 presidential elections saw three campaigns by prominent South Asian Americans; Nikki Haley, Vivek Ramaswamy and, of course, vice-president Kamala Harris.

In 2024 the majority of US cricketers, and the vast majority of cricket fans come from the South Asian diaspora. This has meant some readjustment for the ethnic groups who have traditionally run the game in the country – the second- and third-generation Caribbean migrants. Indeed, one of the constant undercurrents on this odyssey has been the niggles between these two groups. Often these have been brushed under the carpet and pooh-poohed. But occasionally tensions have been aired in front of us.

We saw this at the 2006 Under-19s World Cup in Sri Lanka where the US were competing for the first time. Team manager on that jaunt was Ashok Patel, who complained loudly that none of the kids from his own academy had been selected. 'It's because the director in the Atlantic region only favoured his own boys – they're from Guyana,' he insisted. 'Basil Butcher was elected as a coach of the Atlantic region; he got it because he's Guyanese and they're Guyanese. From the president to the majority of the directors to the majority of the selectors – all Guyanese.'

Meanwhile Butcher, who was the squad's trainer, didn't like the Asian players in the squad speaking their own language. 'We have had over and over again in this tour occasions where the Indians would be speaking Hindi,' he complained. 'Sometimes in the presence of us West Indians, who don't understand a word that they're saying. And we're representing an English-speaking country! I mean we have raised this issue and the unfortunate thing is the manager [Patel] is the chief cook and bottle-washer. He has been the guy who has been leading the chorus in speaking Hindi with the other players. And I have called him on it.'

The creation of a genuine American cricketing culture, which transcends mere ethnicity, would overcome this. However, as Butcher admitted at the time, this was still some way away.

'The US is a bunch of enclaves of people of different nationalities and ethnicities,' he reflected. 'I tell people, when they come from England to the United States, the difference between America and England is that in England black folks and white folks live next to each other and socialise. We don't do any of that in America. The only thing we do together is go to work and then we head back to our separate enclaves. The social part in terms of our intermixing doesn't happen as much in the United States as it does in other parts of the world. From the outside you'd say that New York is a melting pot, blah blah blah. Yes, you're exposed to all kinds of people but when you go home you're surrounded by people like you – period.'

How can this be overcome? Only really if cricket starts to make inroads into the rest of the population, the vast (white) majority that have no ancestral links to the Test-playing nations. Writing in 2024, this sentence seems as fanciful as it did when we started out on this journey two decades ago. And yet over and over we have met ordinary Americans who have had no previous knowledge of the game, but who have caught the bug. Their stories are often the most incredible, and they are often the most enthusiastic about the sport. Converts, after all, are invariably more fervent in their faith than lifelong believers.

Erica Rendler, for example, had had no experience of cricket when she took up the game in her late 20s. She gravitated to the sport via idly surfing the web one day: 'I had already graduated college and played field hockey for UC Berkeley and I was looking for something to do,' she remembered when we spoke to her in 2021. 'I was grinding out my day job and I found an ad on Craigslist one night. I was looking for a softball team or something, casual, just to meet people. And there was an ad for cricket: new players, any skills required. So I emailed the coach Raj Japarti and he wrote back right away. He was really excited. He met with me the next day at Stanford out in the field and he introduced me to the game and everything.'

Her prior knowledge of the game was virtually nil. 'I knew it existed. I think I'd seen it once at Stanford from a distance. I remember seeing them with the helmet on and the bat. I didn't know that it was played more like baseball with fielders. I just saw this guy with the grille on his face kind of looking like a jouster or something. It looked really intimidating when I first saw it.'

Rendler was already versed in a number of sports – field hockey, tennis, baseball – so she was familiar with many of the basic skills of the game. 'Holding the bat was the one thing that didn't match with any of the other grips I was accustomed to. But the movement, the drop step, the catching and the soft hands, the hand-eye coordination: It was all pretty much dialled in with stuff I did even just for fun growing up as a kid.'

'I had played competitive sports all my life and was looking for something fun and it turned into another competitive opportunity for me that I stretched out for another decade or so.'

Erica took that opportunity and ran with it. Within a year or so of taking up the sport she had been called into the USA team for the World Cup qualifiers in Bangladesh in 2011.

'It was a conversation starter for sure,' she laughs. 'I mean at that point I had a lot of friends working in collegiate athletic departments or coaching. But nobody was connected to cricket at all. So they thought it was really cool, especially when I was called up to the US national team. It was "woah". It was a kind of funny joke. "There you go, Rendler, put on the jersey!" It was like, "What is she doing now?" It was this funny thing that became really serious all of a sudden.

'My parents didn't really know what was going on. They would be like, "Why don't you focus on your job? You're grown up. You should get on with your life here." Yet I was having a resurgence of my kid sporting days, going full force with the cricket and putting all of my attention towards that.'

Representing her country in Bangladesh was a profoundly moving experience for Rendler. 'Even still to this day it gives me chills. The whole experience was life-changing. I mean just even in the preparation and all the inoculations you had to get before going. It was something that really pulled me out of my comfort zone and opened my eyes to a spot in the world I probably never would have had any reason to visit. The whole experience surrounding it is what fills my memories – seeing all the big buses and the security guards with their machine guns. It was really neat to go to a place where cricket was a big deal.

'The cricket was challenging. I think I did okay considering. I think at that point just batting not out or trying to stay in was the goal. I remember I got 26 not out against South Africa which was a big victory for me.'

As the only white American in the squad, Rendler was inevitably an outsider to an extent. 'I always felt as if I was the visitor, like this is "their sport" and I'm just here to check it out. Everyone else had such a strong connection to cricket, a multi-generational relationship with it within their family. Whereas mine was like a novelty, I'm here to check it out. I'm going to play hard; I'm a strong competitor. But it was just kind of this fun thing that I was tapping into. Like so many other people I could tell by the looks on their parents' faces or coach's face how much it meant for them to succeed. Whereas for me anything I got out of it was just going to be a cherry on top of the cake.

'I trod lightly in the beginning. I don't just jump into a group. I had my humility and tried to blend in, find out who the leaders are and what the scene is, but at first it was hard to prove myself. It's competitive selections, you're always feeling that there are a bunch of people right behind you that are wanting your spot. There was always that challenge, right up until when I retired from the national team. I felt I had to continue proving to myself that I belonged here and that I wasn't this token mark on the roster.'

* * *

Nate Hays was another American from a non-cricketing background whose heart was captured by the game. Like Rendler, the North Carolina-based writer and commentator was already a sports nut and had played baseball in college on a partial scholarship. 'I grew up with baseball and American football – those were the sports I played as I was growing up. I've always been interested in playing sports and team sports in particular and the dynamic of the team. Then I just also wanted to find something new. So I was already very curious at the time when I discovered cricket.'

This was around the time of the 2015 World Cup. 'I work in IT and a lot of the fellas that I work with are Indian guys and obviously they're massive cricket fans, so they were talking about the World Cup one day and their fantasy cricket teams, so I was like, "What's this fantasy sport?"

'So I started asking them and got the kind of typical "you're not going to like it anyway" introduction. But then a couple of them were happy to show me and one of the guys showed me what everyone in cricket had been recently talking about which was the Wahab Riaz versus Shane Watson spell during that World Cup. He said, "Take a look at this" so I watched that video and I was just amazed.

'It was the aggression and the sheer courage [of Watson] to take it until he got his eye in. They told me he just came in the middle, after sitting around. He just came in and this bowler is on top of his game and you would have been easily able to tell me that he was one of the best bowlers who's ever played the game at the moment. Because that's what he looked like. I loved the intensity of it. He's hitting him in the ribs, he's bouncing it over his head. And then he's finishing his run-up several feet away from him and staring him down and clapping. And I was like, "This is something else!" It's not what I thought cricket was like.'

Like many Americans non-cognisant of the sport, Hays has assumed cricket was a genteel English game populated by gentlemen. 'It's kind of that butt end of a joke all the time. And I knew that cricket had a pretty big history in baseball, but I didn't know exactly how much until later.

But I was like, "Oh this is neat. Let me learn about this a little bit.'"

Hays took an online crash course in the intricacies of the game. 'I had to learn how this game works because nobody was able to explain it to me in a way that made any sense. All of the language is unique, and it seems to me it should have just been retired 100 years ago! I mean "maiden" means multiple things. "Wicket" means multiple things. Just the fact they're still saying "maiden" still seems backward, right? So I would stay up hours and hours in the middle of the night. I couldn't find a way to watch the games so I would just look at ball-by-ball updates, trying to get the hang of this and if I saw something I didn't recognise from the scoresheet I would Google it. That's how I learned the game.'

Like Rendler, Hays soon wanted to play cricket himself. Luckily, living in Raleigh in the mid-2010s, he had plenty of opportunities. 'I Googled local cricket and I emailed a guy and he says, "Hey, we need cricket players." I'm like, "I play baseball, I've never played cricket, do you think I can come out to practice?" And that was Aaman's dad who replied to me, the guy who does commentary with me. So, the first time out playing cricket was for his team and Aaman was 12 years old. And we were throwing a football back and forth half the practice. I think I got to bat when the sun was behind the trees for five minutes. It was incredibly difficult.'

Hays's involvement with the sport deepened during Covid. 'I couldn't play cricket. Couldn't play hockey, which is another sport I like. I needed something to do to keep me busy, to keep me from reading the news at three in the morning, so I made a couple of videos, which kind of went around American cricket circles and I got a lot of people getting in touch and responding to that.'

It was around this time that Emerging Cricket, the website devoted to the associate nations, got in touch with Hays. 'I was already a patron of theirs, so I was already giving them money. I was listening intently to every one of their podcasts and they asked me if I wanted to contribute. I saw myself doing behind-the-scenes graphics for them because I have an art background, and then I came across a video of a sports agent in South Africa talking to one of his clients about how he was moving to the USA because he'd gotten a gig with Major League Cricket and nobody else had broken this news. So, I wrote about it.'

Hays was following in the footsteps of another white American who has become the foremost writer about the sport in the US. Peter Della Penna's trajectory was similarly vertical in that there were a mere four years between encountering the game for the first time and writing about it for the cricketing world's most important online platform *Cricinfo*.

Della Penna had been a sports-mad kid and had dreams of becoming a sports journalist covering the New York Giants or the Yankees. But life took an unusual turn when, as part of his year abroad at his university, he chose to go to Australia. In the summer of 2005.

He got off the plane in Sydney on 21 July to catch an internal flight. 'I had an hour and a half fly-over and at the airport, because I needed something to do, I bought a copy of the *Sydney Morning Herald*,' he remembers. 'On the front page there was a picture of Ricky Ponting and there's blood on his face and the headline says "Bloody Hell! These Poms mean business". It was a recap of the first day's play of the first Test.'

'I'm reading all this stuff and it might as well have been in Chinese. It was like, "What the hell is this?" But I thought, "Right, this is on the front page of one of the major international newspapers in Australia and if I'm going to be here for the next six months I should probably learn some more about this sport if I'm going to fit in."'

Della Penna had stumbled upon what many regard as the greatest, the most exciting Test series of the last 50 years, maybe even of all time.

'So that night we went to a hostel and I remember it was all people were talking about. You couldn't avoid it.

You could pick out some stuff fairly easily – how a wicket fell, for example. Shane Warne took one and everyone went berserk. And they celebrated like it was the final night of the World Series. Everyone was hugging each other and running about and high-fiving and jumping up and down. I was like, "This is pretty awesome!" Every time someone gets out it's like this? I could figure out that some stuff is straightforward like a wicket and if someone hit the ball into the ground and it went to the boundary it's a four. And it was obvious when a wicket fell because of the stumps. And they catch it just like baseball.'

In between the first and second Tests Della Penna did some reading up and Googling. But much of his knowledge came from a chance encounter with an Australian kid who had wandered into his apartment (which he shared with four other Americans).

'It was the night before the second Test at Edgbaston and he was just staying with someone in the apartment for the night. I asked him, "Do you know anything about cricket?" He's like, "Yeah, what do you want to know?" So for the next two hours he answered anything I can think of – what's a maiden?

'What's the difference between a wicket out and a wicket partnership? It's like three or four meanings of the word wicket and what do they all mean? What is the difference between swing and seam bowing? What's an off-spinner?

'Soon it was about 1am. And he was like "Mate, I'm so wasted, I need to go to bed" and he just passed out on the couch and I went upstairs and I never saw him again. The first and only time I saw him. It was like one of these great mythical characters and encounters, someone who I met by chance and came through and gave me wisdom and then disappears forever.'

The 2005 Ashes series changed Della Penna's life forever. When he returned to university in Nebraska, he was determined to start playing the sport. An attempt to set up a university cricket club didn't get very far. Then he contacted Omaha Cricket Club and phoned their vice-captain and motivating force Bhaskar Setti.

'I introduce myself. "I'm really interested in playing cricket," blah blah blah. "And you're an American. We don't have any Americans come out and play. Have you ever played before?" I say, "I've played in parks in Australia and stuff but I've never actually played in a formal match." He says [sternly], "We take our cricket very seriously. We play serious cricket." I say, "I know. That's why I want to join. I'm looking for something like that. I want to play in an organised match. I'm fairly athletic and I'm sure I could pick up things if I'm given an opportunity. I know I haven't played in an organised match but I'd like to learn and get better." "Well, we have a tournament coming up this weekend. You can't play in it, because all the teams are already set but if you want to, come and watch."

'The day arrives and it was rainy and there was nobody there. So I call Bhaskar and say, "What happened? I thought there was a match going on?" He says, "Well we cancelled the tournament because there is a forecast for rain this week." "When's the next match?" "We have a match next weekend. Do you want to play?" "Yeah, I want to play." "I'll try and get you in." He tells me the match is going to start at eight in the morning.'

Peter was so excited he could hardly sleep the night before. He arrived at the ground with only two to three hours' rest, but in good time at 7.30am. Nobody was there. Half an hour drifted by. Still, nobody turned up. By 8.15 the ground was still empty. 'This is getting stupid. I get back in my car and I'm ready to drive up off when, all of a sudden, this guy pulls up in a Porsche and it's Bhaskar. He gets out and introduces himself and says, "Hey, you know sometimes the guys are a little late getting to the ground."'

That was an understatement. It took until 11am for both teams to assemble. 'They sent me in to bat at eight I think. I pushed this thing on to mid-off. I had my first run and then came back and a couple of balls later I got bowled by a yorker and I was devastated.

'But going into the field I said, "Put me anywhere where the ball is going to go – I'm a really good fielder and can catch anything." So a 6ft square guy gets a full ball and he hooks it and it comes straight to me. I get down and I take it! And everyone looks at me like they're shocked. Like, "Yeah, what is this American doing? How did he just catch like that? He's never played before." It took about five to ten seconds and then they all come running in and congratulating me. I was doing what I'd seen on TV, throwing into the air and then everybody goes nuts. Then everybody is like, "Okay, this guy is good enough to stay."'

In his own words, it took a long time for Peter to feel accepted on the team. But he stuck it out, and improved. Eventually it was time to head home to New Jersey, which meant trying to get a cricket team in the Garden state.

'I went to this Labor Day match in August 2008 in Bloomfield, near Newark between this church team called St Vincents and a team called the Bermuda All Stars. There were all these West Indian people having this big party – they're all drinking and talking about Obama. I started watching and I was the only white guy at the ground, so people were like, "Are you Australian? Are your parents Australian?" "No, I'm American." "No, where were you born?" "Carolina." "No, where were your parents born?"

'I asked about playing and contacted the club co-ordinator in February/March. He says, "Hey, we got a meeting in a couple of weeks." "Okay, keep me updated." I call him up and he says, "Yeah, we got a meeting, all the club is going to be there. Be there at seven o'clock."

'I get there at 6.45pm and I'm the first person there. It's 7.15, 7.30 and one or two guys show up. I'm starting to get itchy. "What's going on here? Is there a meeting or isn't there?" "Yeah, yeah there is – just be patient." So 8/8.15 comes around and we're just sitting there shooting the breeze, not really discussing anything proper about the club and then it was, "Alright, let's start the meeting" and we just talked for about five minutes about nothing and then it was, "Alright, let's go." A total waste of time.'

The meeting was reorganised for the following week, only for the same thing to happen again. Two weeks passed by and Peter gets a call from his contact asking him if he's available for the first game of the season.

'He said, "We're going to have a match on a Saturday, but it's not going to be set until I know we got a lot of players. We'll call you back and let you know it's on for sure." So that was Wednesday. By Friday he's like, "I don't know yet. Give me two hours." I call back in a bit and ask again if the match is on. "We won't know until tomorrow morning. You will have to go to the ground to find out." Is it or isn't it? He's like, "Oh, there's going to be a match."

'I get to the ground for 9.15am and there is already two matches going on. I recognise some of the guys from the meetings, so I go over and ask are we playing or not?' "No man, these guys got here before us. We'll have to wait until they are finished." We waited until about 1.30pm/2pm and the first game finishes and I ask the other guys whether we can go on but we don't have enough players. "Why don't we have 11?" "Well, we got some phone calls from guys and they asked if the match was on and we told them no because there are guys already here. They were going to come but when we told them the match was later they decided to stay at home so now we don't have 11." It was just the stupidest thing ever. A waste of an entire day.'

His patience severely tested, Peter went back to the drawing board and the Garden State League website. 'I think I wrote 15 or 20 emails out to club secretaries. I didn't get a single reply. So I thought, "This is stupid. I'm going to call a few people." So I called this guy called Kalpesh Patel whose club played their games in Far Hills and he told me I couldn't join their club as they had too many members and I'd never get the chance to play.'

Instead Kalpesh recommended a team that he knew needed players. Peter rang them and left a message. No one got back to him. He phoned Kalpesh again, who suggested simply going down to the ground at a time when they were playing and introducing himself.

'It's just 11 Gujarati guys speaking Gujarati to each other and not wanting to talk to me at all. I tried to start a conversation with someone and they'd just give me these one-word answers and then they'd go back to speaking Gujarati to each other.'

Peter then tried another local club, Edison, and even took part in a few net sessions. But then when the question of membership came up, the ranks started closing once more. 'One time the captain and the vice-captain were there and they were like, "Oh yeah, you're really good. I think we could really use you." And I said, "What's your club membership like? I like the sound of your club." And they're like, "Oh well we need to have, er, a meeting of the club general committee before we can accept members so we'll give you a call."'

A couple of weeks go by and Peter raises the question of joining once more: 'I say "I'm really eager to play. Can I play? I'd like to join. I can pay membership fees. I just want to play. What do I have to do?" "Oh well, the club committee still hasn't met regarding new players and we'll be having a meeting this Wednesday so once that happens we'll let you know."

'So another week goes by and I don't hear anything. On Tuesday I get an email from the club secretary. "Dear Peter, I hear you're interested in playing. At this current time we have set rosters for both our Saturday and Sunday teams and we don't think we can accept any new players *but* we recognise the fact that you are a player with great potential and has special circumstances. However, we can't guarantee you that you will actually get to play any games. But we are willing to offer you the chance to play at least two matches and if you prove yourself then you might get a regular slot in the team. But in order to play the two matches you will need to join the club and the membership fees are $150. You don't get to play any matches until the fee is paid. $150 will get you an invitation to any Edison Cricket Club social events including the year-end Edison Cricket Club awards banquet."'

For Della Penna, the simple process of finding a cricket club was akin to a fantastical quest, full of obstacles and trap doors, where one's progress is constantly stalled without the possession of some arcane knowledge that is seemingly forever just out of reach. Cricketing skills are not enough – you need the patience of a saint and the hide of a rhino. 'You really have to be hardcore to try and get involved with cricket in this country,' he admits.

'But you hear these same people say, "We can't wait! We want cricket to grow in America. We want it to get into the mainstream. We want to get people involved, we want so many people playing cricket!" And then when someone presents themselves it's like: "Wait ... so you are an American? You can't be an American. Americans don't play this game. We've never had an American play this game." They are resistant and it's almost like they are resistant on purpose. They are not willing to accept that an American actually wants to participate.'

And this is the irony. A large portion (though not all) of the South Asian and Caribbean diaspora hug the game close, as a comfort, a relic of their old lives in the old country. It's part of their identity. And why should they give that up? But to grow in the US, cricket will, at some point, have to be shared if it is to make its way out of the ghetto. 'They feel like it's "our" game,' says Della Penna. 'Instead of it being considered everyone's game. It's "ours". "Our" game that you can't be a part of and you can't play.'

So how can that change? The example of soccer proves that it's not impossible for a sport once utterly marginal in the States to make inroads into the mainstream. But soccer's journey has been fitful, and the subject of major investment a number of times both from private sources (NASL) and from the world governing body (1994 men's World Cup).

And the whole world plays soccer – walk into a bar in any major American city during a World Cup and they'll be showing a game. Not so with cricket.

'There are very few opportunities for the mainstream American to observe a good game of cricket,' reflects Dream Cricket's Venu Palaparthi. 'Maybe it was back in the day – if it was on ESPN and they had nothing better to do. But these days it's all pay per view, streaming websites and it's member only, right? For us to think that somehow Joe Smith is suddenly going to discover cricket and suddenly going to get attracted to it is impossible.'

Palaparthi suggests starting off with schools and praises the work of the United States Youth Cricket Association. His notion is that the exoticism, the other-ness of cricket could actually be a selling point.

'I think if you look at cricket it's still seen as an expat sport unfortunately and now it is increasingly seen as an Indian sport, or a South Asian expat sport. So we have gone in the wrong direction, right? We went from the glory days of Philadelphia Cricket Club when it was an all-American sport with JB King to this thing that brown people play and just them. Now how do we turn it around? There are no other options but to take the Bollywood or a yoga view of these things. Yoga started off as this thing that South Asians do, but now it's mainstream. Every block in New

York you're going to has a yoga studio. Bollywood dancing – same story. Cuisine – the same story, right? There is a biryani cart on every street corner in New York.

'There is an increasing acceptance of things that are still thought of as very ethnic or culturally distinct from us but that's okay. Let's take those people who are curious, bring them in first and grow from there, right?'

Another route might be a new venture that is a collaboration between two figures from the world of professional baseball and dissidents from USA Cricket. If it's successful (and as ever in the world of US cricket that's a big if) it stands a fighting chance of taking the game out into the American heartlands.

North American Cricket Club is an attempt to encourage baseball or softball players who haven't made it to professional sport to take their existing skills and adapt them to cricket, in the same way that Erica Rendler has. It's the brainchild of Nick Corso and Kameron Loe, who have both worked in baseball for decades, most recently as vice-president and president of APBPA (Association of Professional Ball Players of America). They've teamed up with Julien Fountain, an ex-British Olympic baseball player, who's worked as a coach in both sports, as well as Julie Abbott and Jamie Lloyd, erstwhile board members from USA Cricket.

We met Nick Corso via Zoom early in January 2025 and he seems full of enthusiasm for a project that is reliant on a hunch. 'It's a bat and ball sport,' he explains. 'It's hand-eye coordination and I think we can add a North American sport structure around the sport of cricket. It was a popular sport in the United States prior to it actually being the United States and we kind of lost the sport. We always referred to cricket as the grandfather of baseball in the United States and we hope to bring that sport back.'

Corso's hunch is that the athletes that have been discarded by pro baseball will want to make the leap to an adjacent sport. 'I work with a lot of athletes at all ages and, especially when it comes to boys' baseball, there are some kids who are drafted into Minor League Baseball right out of high school that are great talents but never get a chance to actually make it to the big league. I know a lot of those guys who played independently in Minor League Baseball for the love of the game and who will stay in the competition, literally making no money for eight to ten years because they love the game.

'We're hoping to draw from the collegiate marketplace right now as we understand that the women play softball in college. They really have no career path if they continue professional sport after they graduate. So, we hope to provide them with a career path in the sport of cricket.

I know so many female college softball players and male baseball players that are just tremendous athletes. Either they're not playing or they can't play in the big league for one reason or another, so it's an opportunity to take their skills and transfer them over to the sport of cricket.'

The initial idea is for men's and women's professional leagues. At present Corso is in the process of setting up the teams – there will be eight initially in each league. This summer there will be clinics where prospective players can try out the sport and see if it takes their fancy. Following that there are try-outs, regional training camps where the new players can sharpen their skills, a combine and finally, by the end of the year, a draft whereby the players will be allocated their new teams.

And he has plans to document all this as it happens, for a prospective documentary: 'We're positioning it as "*Ted Lasso* meets *Welcome To Wrexham*", he says. Indeed, the documentary is central to Corso's idea of taking cricket to the US mainstream. 'It would follow the start-up of the league and then after the first phase of the documentary there are so many challenges that people would love to see – all the negotiations; dealing with people who own facilities, how we recruit players, how we bring in sponsorship. All this stuff that happens behind the scenes is pretty intriguing.'

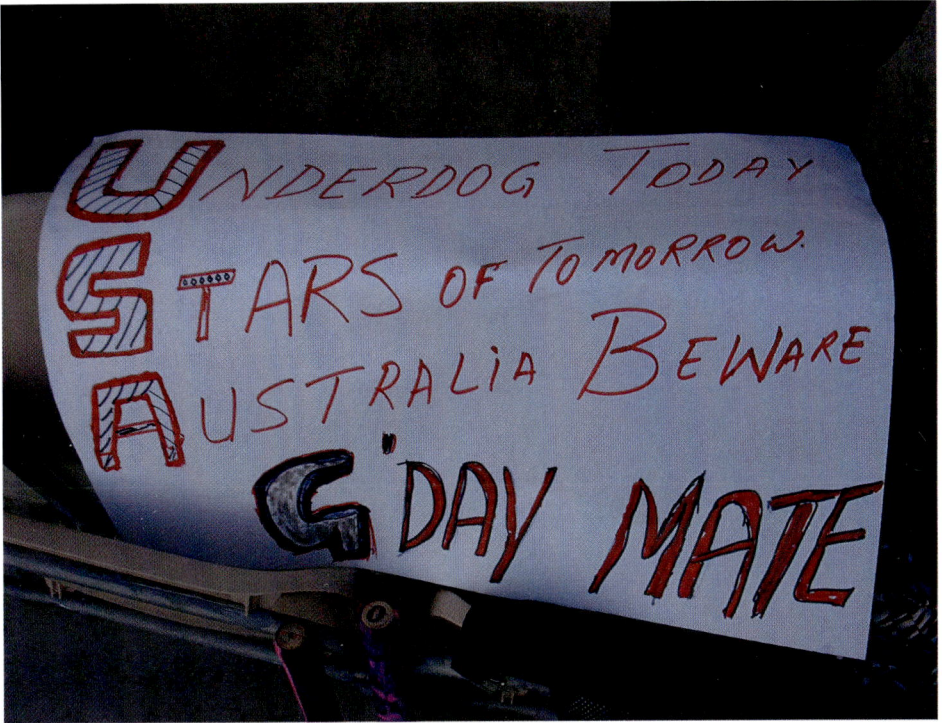

A USA supporter's hopeful placard, Rose Bowl, September 2004. Gentlemen of Philadelphia

The mat and wicket at Haverford College

Philadelphia Cricket Club from the air (courtesy of Philadelphia CC)

Philadelphia CC. At home with the Homies

Ted Hayes shows his team how to run (courtesy of Rich Grove/Fellow Traveller)

Team practice in Compton (courtesy of Rich Grove/Fellow Traveller)

Ted instructs the team before the game (courtesy of Rich Grove/Fellow Traveller)

Theo and Isaac Hayes perform the Hip Hop cricket rap (courtesy of Rich Grove/Fellow Traveller)

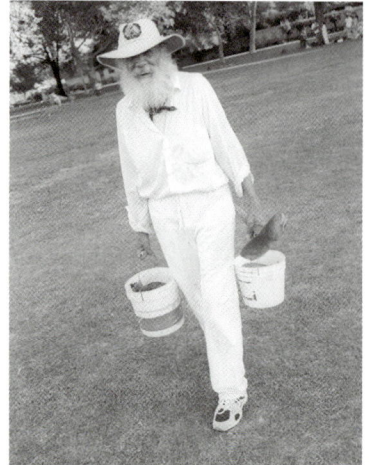

Clifford Severn (courtesy of Rich Grove/Fellow Traveller)

Compton Homies and Pops on tour in England 2001 (courtesy of Rich Grove/ Fellow Traveller)

The field at Staten Island CC. The Cricket Junkies. The Long And Winding Road

Steve Messiah bats for the USA against Australia, September 2004

Clayton Lambert – ex-West Indies international turned US player and then coach, 2010

From left to right: Kevin Darlington, Sorab Warma and Sushil Nadkarni warm up for the game against Scotland, UAE, February 2010

Usman Shuja is held aloft by his teammates Carl Wright, Imran Awan and Steve Messiah after he takes a wicket (courtesy cricket europe)

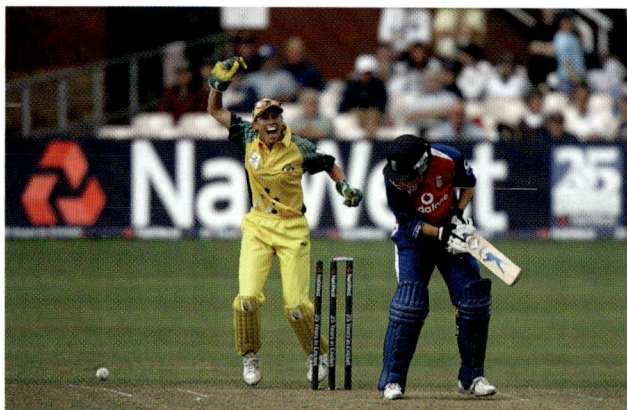

Julia Price in her playing days, representing Australia (AP photo)

Batsman Sakthi Kandaswaamy of Auburn University practises with his team at Broward County stadium, Lauderhill, March 2010

Fans at the Minor League game at Church St Park between Morrisville Raptors and New Jersey Stallions, August 2022

Erica Rendler (courtesy of Erica Rendler)

Iain Higgins – ICC chief operating officer who later became USA Cricket's first CEO

Seattle Orcas and MI New York flags – given out at the first Major League final, 2023

Aaron Jones and Monank Patel after USA beat Canada in their opening game at the 2024 T20 World Cup

USA celebrate the dismissal of Mohammad Rizwan – USA v Pakistan, June 2024, T20 World Cup

Saurabh Netravalkar celebrates after the greatest result in US cricket history – beating Pakistan in June 2024

He cites the example of the NFL docu-series, *Hard Knocks*. 'You follow a team from pre-season into the training throughout the season. It's a very human story because maybe in our division there's a female athlete who has graduated from college who is engaged to be married and she has to say to her fiancé, "I know we're going to plan to be married, I know I was going to go on to my career over here, *but* I have an opportunity to continue and be a professional in this brand new league and I'd like to give that a shot." So, you'd follow that human dynamic story along with the progress of the team in try-outs, people making the team, people not making the team.'

Corso is aware that cricket remains a tough sell to US mainstream media. 'We tend to have myopia here in North America, right? Our sports are wonderful. But it's hard to get people to understand that cricket has 2.5 billion fans worldwide. In comparison our baseball has 400 million – it pales in comparison to the global culture of cricket.'

At the time of writing, NACC is scheduled to launch in 2026. The finance isn't there yet – Corso says that he's reluctant to go down the route of using private equity and running the risk of losing control of the project. If not, there's also the possibility of crowdfunding and selling ownership rights to the teams in the same way the Green Bay Packers have in American football. Neither are there any owners of the teams yet. Corso said he'd be open to current holders of US baseball or football franchises owning a team. As for team owners outside the US, 'We haven't delved too deeply into that.'

Could NACC be the vehicle that starts cricket's drive (back) into the US sporting heartland? In its favour is the fact it's headed by two people who know the unique sporting landscape of North America like the back of their hand. When asked if it's possible, Corso is positive: 'Absolutely it can happen.'

The next couple of years will reveal just how many other Erica Rendlers there are out there and answer the question of whether NACC is a genuine game-changer or if Corso and Loe are just another pair of dreamers.

10

A Field in an Infertile Land

Cricket in America's remote outposts

FAR AWAY from the coasts and the huge urban centres there is another country, another America. Whether you term this as the 'heartland' or 'flyover country' matters not. Most visitors to the United States never set foot there. And attempting to find cricket in states like Nebraska, Wyoming, Idaho, Iowa or Kansas is nothing but a fool's errand. Isn't it?

And yet cricket has made inroads into even these places. Indeed, it is played in virtually every state in the mainland United States. Up among the great plains of North Dakota where playing the sport is unthinkable for most of the year, there is – would you believe it? – a Fargo Cricket Club. Several hundred miles to the south there is a Sioux Falls Cricket Club in South Dakota. Cricket has been played in Hawaii since the 19th century and Honolulu

CC can boast that it is the oldest sporting club in all of the Pacific Islands.

Wherever there are expats, and in particular expats from South Asia, there is cricket and this silent migration that has occurred as the tech industry has grown in prominence over the last 30 years has been the main driver. But even then cricket doesn't sprout up automatically – these are still largely unpromising, barren lands. You also need a few determined individuals in each of these out-of-the-way areas to make the calls, book the pitches, source the equipment and *nurture* a cricketing ecosystem.

Kansas City

Maulik Nanavati relocated to the US at the dawn of the 21st century; initially to California, but within a year he had settled further east, to the state that geographically is slap bang in the middle of the country: Kansas.

'I moved from India and had played at various levels back there, at college in Mumbai and in a couple of leagues,' he remembers. 'But when I arrived here in 2001 there were only three teams. Soon after I moved there was a big tournament. There is a big university here in Kansas City, a lot of students come from different countries, mainly Asian students. They organised this charity tournament and I formed a team. It was a case of "I know you, do you know somebody else?" and "Hey, do you want to play, you want to play?" So when we had the first game, 20 minutes before the game we met at the ground. I only knew one or two people on that team, right? Cricket in Kansas? Let's go.'

Maulik's ad hoc XI actually won that day. They never played together again, but Maulik – an opening bowler – was quickly recruited by one of the three teams there that did play regularly, for whom he still plays today: Friends XI.

Initially the three teams played occasional games with a tennis ball. Gradually the game in Kansas developed. 'So after we had been playing tennis ball cricket for a few years, our team took the initiative and said, "Hey guys, some of us have played hard-ball in India. How about we try this?" So we started a hard-ball league in 2004, the MWCL – the Midwest Cricket League.

'Again initially it was three or four teams, then six to eight teams. We struggled a bit to go beyond eight teams for a while. But in 2015 or so we had another good influx of immigrant population into the town. For the last T20 tournament we did in the fall of 2024 we had three divisions of eight teams so about 24 teams.'

The Midwest Cricket League depends heavily on the constant influx of migrants from cricket-playing nations. But even then, convincing people to commit to the game is hard. 'A lot of people are here with young kids and jobs in a foreign country, family situations and all that. So time is a factor. Cost is also a factor because hard-ball cricket is not cheap. Nobody is paying you, but we have to pay rent for the ground. We order the cricket balls and gear from other countries, though that isn't so much of a problem now with the internet.'

The other big challenge is finding grounds in a culture that is barely aware of cricket and its unique requirements. 'We had a ground for a good ten years after we started in 2004,' laments Maulik. 'But then soccer is growing so much here in the US and the city decided to build a huge soccer complex there, so we lost that.

'We found another place – we have a ground about an hour and a half drive from here. Then later on we found a free ground, but it would have added two and a half hours of drive time for everybody at weekends. You imagine the cost of gas for five or six cars going per team. So everyone decided it's okay to pay $200 for a ground nearer if it saves two and a half hours for so many people.'

There is also the residual costs. 'We have to hire a guy to mow the lawn. On one ground they do that but we have to pay extra because the city only does it to a certain specification. For cricket purposes we need it slightly shorter. There are a couple of times in a year like spring or fall when it's growing so much so you might have to cut it back twice in a bid to go to that specification. So, we have to make a budget for that.'

The MCL compares well to other leagues, he explains, but if any players show the sort of talent that might interest a Minor or Major League team, they quickly leave. It would help if Kansas had its own Minor League team, but the nearest one is a three-hour drive away in St Louis.

Women's cricket, he says, is 'in its infancy' here. He is more hopeful about youth development – there is a Kansas Cricket Youth Academy: 'That's been going for ten years now,' Maulik explains. 'So some of the kids that first started going there when they were seven or eight years old are now 15 or 16 and playing in the MCL. They're by no means the finished product. But I think it's just a matter of time that one of those kids plays in the Minor or Major League.'

If there's hope for the development of the game in the state, it's what he remembers from his youth in India. 'Growing up there, cricket was at a certain level until the 1990s. It was only when it started to go into the smaller places in the 2000s that it exploded. If your talent pool is only coming from Mumbai and Delhi you'll find players but you won't have the depth that the bigger countries have. I think that's what needs to happen in the US as well, which will help both the top of US cricket and places like Kansas. There's interest in the urban places and the big centres, but it needs to trickle down to places like Kansas and Kentucky and Iowa and Minneapolis, all these places that also have a big immigrant population.'

Minneapolis, Minnesota

Maulik's frustrations are echoed by many working in the women's game throughout the US. But those challenges – a small player pool, lack of infrastructure – are especially acute in areas off the beaten track.

Kalaivani Gunasekaran runs the women's cricket programme in Minneapolis, Minnesota, which at present has around 20 players. 'We are slowly getting the interest,' she smiles. 'Of those 20 there will be drop-outs each year and newcomers so we practise on the field, mostly on the football or the baseball field. Our season is only really four months from May to September. For the rest of time, we practise indoors in the nets.'

The Minnesota team are part of the current US women's pathway. Every year they compete against teams from St Louis, Atlanta and North Carolina to see who will represent the Central zone. 'North Carolina and Atlanta teams have won for so long,' says Kalaivani. 'And North Carolina is the hub where they have a number of national players. I would say we are progressing slowly. I can see the improvement year by year from when we started in 2021, compared to now.'

Kalaivani receives, in her own words, 'very little' assistance in this from the governing body. 'There is some guidance provided by them but still it's not like someone can come and coach us or lead us for a few sessions. And we get nothing in terms of financial assistance because of the travel and the cost associated with it. Although we have 20 players that are focused and ready to travel, there are others that are still not certain about spending that much time and money. If you have kids or you're working, there are so many things that get in the way.'

And facilities are all too often a problem: 'We have 10 to 12 grounds but most of the time they are occupied by men's cricket. There is one dedicated cricket facility that started last year. Until then we had to book baseball cages to practice, and they don't have a proper run-up length.

'I love the job but having said that I do get frustrated sometimes. It's things like players' commitment. Because of the domestic pathway we have laid out a plan but there are always last-minute drop-outs – that kind of stuff. But I am optimistic. Thinking of where we started and where we are, things are definitely improving.'

Boise, Idaho

Nestling in the foothills of the Rocky Mountains lies the town of Boise (pronounced Boy-see), the capital of Idaho.

And yes, even here, in what at first may seem like an unpromising environment there is cricket.

There is just one club though – Boise CC. Like Kansas, cricket started here around the turn of the millennium. Omair Shamim though has few of the frustrations of Maulik. Just to be able to play the sport at any level in a relatively small place like Boise is an achievement.

Omair moved there in 1998 from Pakistan where he had been at medical school ('I might have ended up playing cricket professionally, but my studies took up too much of my time,' he claims). On arriving in the US, he found just tennis-ball cricket in Boise. 'We tried to form a group of like-minded folks and we started playing with the regular ball. We used to play at a local school. Then in about 2000–01 we gathered and started playing at Timberline High School.'

'There was no pitch there. There was nothing, just a ground and a concrete pathway that goes between the two grounds, so big areas. We just took a mat and laid it over and that became our pitch.'

Around 2008 things began to get more serious. 'We asked Boise Park and Recreation if they would give us a place to play cricket. So we met with the officials. They asked us, "Give us a proposal. What do you want to do and how do you want to do it?" In 2008 Boise CC formed and

I and a couple of others met with officials. We saw one that was in a neighbourhood where there were a few roads nearby and we were worried that we had a couple of players who hit pretty hard and the ball would end up in the houses.

'So we turned it down and then they offered us a ground, shared by lacrosse and soccer. We worked among ourselves, so four or five people contributed about $1,000 each at that time and laid down the pitch. We hired a contractor. We dug up the place and laid down the pitch in spring 2009 and then started our first official league in Boise.'

At present the league, and indeed Boise CC as a whole, comprises 'four or five teams and around 60 players'. With such a small number the club have introduced a couple of rules to make sure there is fair competition in their mini league. First, they have an NFL-style draft every season to make sure one team doesn't snaffle all the best players. They have also put in place an intriguing in-play rule to ensure teams are more evenly matched.

'We have a rule of seven,' Omair explains. 'So each player is given a number from one to five. So if you're five it means you're one of best. And two you are ordinary, trying to learn the game and so on. So the rule of seven means that until 13 overs only two players with a combination of seven can play together. So not only all good players go up and utilise all the overs and players who are not that good do not have a chance to play. So a four and a three can play together. But if a two and five are playing together and the two gets out you cannot replace him with another five, only a number two. It means those players get more opportunities to bat.

'The same with bowling. Each team has to use at least seven bowlers and at least two overs must be bowled by number two bowlers. Not everybody is a very good player and we want to have participation because people start to drop off if they come all day and then they don't have a chance to play. Who wants to field for 20 overs? That's no fun.'

Cricket in Boise was also given a boost when the tech firm Micron – one of the biggest employers in the town – created a field specifically for cricket a couple of years back. 'We now have a lush green and a very good even thin grass and we can do ground shots,' smiles Omair. Indeed, free of the worry of losing their grounds that other cricket clubs have elsewhere, he seems confident about the future of the game in Idaho.

'It all depends upon the workforce in Micron, because they are our main employer,' he suggests. When we ask about the prospect of fewer work visas under the new Trump administration, he pulls down the shutter: 'I don't want to go into the political situation. But I don't think that we will be affected too much ... though maybe in the future we might have less of an influx of folks.'

If there are challenges, they are merely the same as any amateur sports club wherever they are in the world – finding people to do stuff. 'Each year we have difficulty finding volunteers. The club is run by an executive committee, and we have elections every two years. But we have had no nominations this year and we are trying to find folks who want to do it.'

But even then those who commit to volunteering could easily find themselves leaving Boise. 'It's such a small place that people are here with their employment. If you lose your employment, you go out of the state to find a new job. There are less opportunities here and it's a barrier for people to come in. We have had some great players, really committed folks who were here, but lost their jobs or got a better opportunity out of state and went to California and now they're playing there in their league.'

Anyone who's tried to run a cricket club in a small town would doubtless nod their head in recognition. Some problems are universal.

Omaha, Nebraska

Twelve hundred or so miles to the south lies Omaha, the largest city in Nebraska. Cricket here has been present for longer, since the early 1990s, but arguably its development has been slower, much to the annoyance of Bhaskar Setti, the Indian expat who has been at the heart of Omaha cricket for over two decades.

'Cricket was born in our city much further back than Kansas City and all the bigger cities around us like Des Moines or Cedar Rapids. We put the flag in first in 1991 whereas they [Kansas City] started in around 2003. Now since then immigration has grown in Kansas City and they have grown bigger than us because they started figuring out how to approach the cities because of the technology and everything. They approached the city governments successfully so they got funding and even more people came in. Omaha is still struggling with all these issues.'

Bhaskar came here in 1997: 'Placed in the middle of the country where there is snow and no immigrant population, no Commonwealth countries population where they played cricket.' His years here have left him with an intriguing hybrid Indian-American accent, and it's clear that he has absorbed many of the aspects of his adoptive country's culture, most notably a can-do positivism.

'I started thinking about creating my own cricket environment,' he explains. 'So I reached out to people who were already playing cricket, but in a more unorganised way. Back then we had to get all the equipment from India

– there's no online, there are no local shops selling cricket gear. And since it's a cold part of the country it's very hard to have a dirt pitch. It's a lot of rolling, it's very costly and we don't have visas other than work visas – we are supposed to work in our jobs rather than focusing on developing sports around here. It was only after ten years, when we were comfortable with our immigration status and knew nobody was going to throw us out of the country, that we got into the sport.'

In the early days even scraping together 11 players was problematic. 'There were only a limited number of people playing. When I came here it was motel owners and agricultural doctors – this is farming country. There was no Facebook at that time, no way of communicating other than phone calls. It was a matter of going to a party and dragging people out, saying, "Come on man, come and play cricket tomorrow." Some people who are not even cricketers were forced into playing, just to keep it going – that's how I did it anyway.

'Later on Yahoo groups, technology came in and communication got a little easier. But mostly it was socialising, finding somebody, asking them questions. "Have you played cricket back in India? Back in Sri Lanka? Why don't you come and play? If we play, city government is not going to take away the field from us."'

Bhaskar formed Omaha Cricket Club, later renaming it Omaha Cricket Association 'to make it more Americanised'. Essentially it works as an umbrella organisation for the teams that play in the city. Last year, seven took part in the hard-ball summer league whilst 12 took part in an indoor league during autumn 2024.

Right up to 2010, he says it was a 'matter of survival'. After then immigration started to increase, and cricket managed to take more of a foothold in the town. 'The companies started hiring and the economy has grown. Not only doctors and motel owners and agricultural scientists, but people from the IT industry – slowly people have started coming.'

He started to spread the word about cricket by touring the local schools. 'I introduced cricket into 50 schools in the area. I started donating cricket kits to small kids in elementary schools, middle schools and high schools, though in high schools they used to ridicule my accent. I didn't care.

'But elementary and middle school coaches were embracing our sport as a new sport because my approach was that cricket has some great advantages. In baseball you hit and you run without any partners. In cricket it takes teamwork to make a run. I made the point of mentioning the history – that Abraham Lincoln played cricket, Washington's troops played cricket in Valley Forge. America's first sport was cricket, not baseball or anything else. I really tried to make it a patriotic thing for them.' Later on Bhaskar linked up with Jamie Harrison's USYCA to continue his schools programme.

He explains that the main challenges in building cricket in Nebraska are twofold – one is the facilities. After scrabbling round for years to find decent grounds Bhaskar built a field in Dodge Park, right up against the River Missouri. 'We spent $250,000 to build a cricket field. Unfortunately, every three or four years the river floods and last year all our investment was gone. We put in new seed last winter. It's growing. But it's a struggle as every two or three years it is completely washed out.' The only alternative is a pitch that has been constructed on top of a disused landfill site. 'The ball comes up and hits you on the nose. So many times the ambulance has carried players away. Some teams don't care.

'Developing cricket here is like growing a plantation in a desert. It's tough. But the love in this part of the world for cricket is far more than in cities. You don't have to do much in cities. There is a much larger population that play cricket, a lot of businesses that want their attention, so they sponsor. It's easy.

'Here it is such a big struggle,' he adds wearily. 'I was able to maintain relationships with the city government officials.

They became a part of my family, mingling with them for 25 years, attending their Christmas parties, wishing their kids happy birthdays, creating a certain sense of family to get something out of it and build something in cricket, otherwise the cricket community can't afford to survive in this part of the country alone.'

The other challenge is immigration, or rather the knowledge that the fate of Nebraskan cricket is tied to the continued flow of expats from South Asia. 'Even though it is more than 20 years it's still dependent on immigration. And not too many people come here. Those that do have no time to go and teach a kid. Nobody has enough money to create infrastructure to build a school team. When people come, they're coming on work visas. They have to put up 40 hours of time in their offices otherwise they lose their visas.'

And even these are looking precarious given the new Trump administration's antipathy to immigration. 'It's concerning,' says Bhaskar. 'What if college visas are taken away? What if H1B1 work visas are limited? It's going to affect our cricket. But what can you do? We are used to the river flooding. We are used to handling other problems. This is one more problem. We know how to live with what we have.'

But you sense that Bhaskar (and others in his position) thrive on this adversity. 'Cricket here is altogether a different animal. Cricket here is community development, not competition. Well, it is competition, but it is also a community.

'I have got so many people jobs. I have got so many people homes. I am like a big brother almost, a father who is not here with them. Every time something happens in their lives – "Oh my wife is not letting me play, Bhaskar. She wants me to wash dishes on Saturday before going out." – I respond, "Yeah, you have to work because this game takes four to five hours, so you have to pay your dues as a husband and then come here and play. That's how it goes." Every time I despair, I think, "I have a lot of friends, I have mentored over 200 guys. They are spread all over the country. They still call me with their personal problems, they still call me with their cricket problems. Sometimes I wish I could have done something for the sport at a bigger level, but I justify that by saying that I touched their lives.

'So it's on entirely different animal from the cities. I have heard from so many friends, "Why are you in a place where your passion is wasted?" But I like to develop here, cultivating a field in an infertile land, as opposed to a city. If you can create cricket here, you can develop cricket anywhere in the world.'

11

The Journey Home

US cricket post USACA. Major League arrives –
and the T20 World Cup

THERE WAS a certain irony that at the same time as the US military was spending hundreds of billions of dollars occupying and 'nation building' in Afghanistan, US cricket was in the embarrassing position of being subject to an occupying force. With its expulsion in July 2017, USACA was removed from power and the ICC Americas team moved in with the intention of building a new body that would be transparent, democratic and able to take its rightful place once more among the top tier of associate nations.

In September 2017 it was announced that the new governing body wouldn't be the existing ACF, but a new body called USA Cricket. By the end of the year, it was announced that a new constitution had been agreed by all parties. It included many of the requirements USACA had previously been dragging their heels on – staggered terms for board members which would all be limited, three independent directors, player representatives on the board and an independent chairman. In addition to this, any changes to the constitution would require a two-thirds majority of the entire membership. The ICC chief executive David Richardson seemed pleased, calling it 'a best practice constitution that gives the new national governing body in the USA the best possible chance of success'.

John Aaron, an old USACA board member who had switched to the ACF, seemed satisfied with the finished constitution and maintained that it would prevent another situation where a Dainty-like figure could assume total control. 'It would be very hard for them to do that given the staggering terms, so there is no collusion or very little chance for collusion,' he told us in 2018. 'I'm sure there will be two or three people who get together with the same ideas and the same agendas to move things in a different direction. But I think you will still need a voting bloc of the majority on the board, so you still need seven votes for a majority of ten.

'There are some checks and balances in place, so I think it is very unlikely that the same thing will happen again. You would have to have at least seven people come together and say, "We can hold up a bloc against the others," and I don't see that happening because I don't see those three independent directors risking their reputation to be embroiled in some incompetently corrupt scenarios. They would have too much to lose.'

Aaron had run for one of the club director positions, but lost out in the end. But Sushil Nadkarni (as league director) was elected, as were Usman Shuja and Nadia Gruny as player representatives. A couple of months later it was announced that Paraag Marathe, the executive vice president of San Francisco 49ers football team, who had also been involved with Leeds United in the UK, had been elected as chairman of the new body.

At the same time as this, things were improving on the field. In November 2018 the national men's team finally won promotion to WCL Division Two when they finished second to hosts Oman in that year's Division Three tournament, winning four games out of five.

Around this time the ICC were going through the process of restructuring (again) the process by which associate nations qualified for the World Cup. So the USA's next tournament – Division Two in Namibia in April 2019 – would be their last as part of the World Cricket League. In the end they did well enough to finish third of out six, beating the hosts by just two runs in a nail-biting opening game as well as Papua New Guinea and Hong Kong. It meant that they – along with the other top associates – were accorded ODI status and would play a series of internationals over the next few years to ascertain who would qualify for the 2023 World Cup.

Then in May 2019 came the news that the new body had partnered with an organisation called American Cricket Enterprises (ACE) to launch a new professional T20 league in 2021. A few months later in February 2020 there was an announcement that in addition to this, ACE and USA Cricket were going to launch a 'minor league' T20 competition in several major cities before Major League launched. This was a positive time for all those who cared about the game in the US. At long last the sunshine seemed to be finally breaking through the clouds. The new dawn that American cricket had long been waiting for had arrived. It seemed.

Then Covid happened. Lockdown. Around the US and around the world cricket fields fell silent as the players stayed at home. The US national team would not play for 18 months and the launches of both Minor and Major Leagues were kicked back to 2022 and 2023 respectively.

Both inside and outside time slowed down. Our own odyssey was put on hold as we grappled with the drama of our own lives back in Europe. When we picked up the trail once more in 2022, the new dawn didn't seem so bright anymore. There were noises to the effect that exactly the same thing was happening with USA Cricket that had happened to USACA.

Usman Shuja remembers that initially he was full of optimism that the new governing body would be able to succeed where its predecessor had failed. 'There was a lot of energy in the board at that time because the ICC had taken over and there was a new constitution. I thought it was a pretty decent set of people to represent and take the game forward.

'I think it was marred by the fact that the whole commercial league – that started to split the board in different ways very quickly. The chair of the board Paraag was leading the structure of the board, but then suddenly someone started to split the board. A couple of people were very disruptive and at that point I heard that it became a bit uncivil as well.'

This was in effect a power struggle between Venu Pisike and Srini Salver (who had replaced Usman as players' representative in February 2020) on one side and Marathe and Iain Higgins on the other. In early 2021 Pisike and Salver sued five fellow board members, including Higgins, alleging that they were changing voting procedures for the next election and thus violating the constitution – these changes included expanding the voting base of USAC members from 725 to nearly 20,000, something that Pisike, with a firm base of members in his Georgia stronghold, was not keen on. Although the suit was later dismissed, it showed that the administrative infighting in US cricket was not a thing of the past.

Then in November 2021, Iain Higgins resigned suddenly, without giving too much of an explanation, though not before delivering the prize that the US had waited decades for. They were going to co-host with the West Indies a World Cup – the T20 event in 2024.

Jamie Lloyd, a coach from New Zealand who had migrated to the US in the early 2010s and begun working with the new body as development manager, remembers the moment well. 'It was bizarre. Iain Higgins called us in the middle of the night. He was in Dubai making the final presentations to head office and they were going to announce and he called us. It was the night before the first day of the men's national championship in 2021. He calls me at 1am and says, "Get up, I've got something I need to tell you guys." We thought, "This is going to be awesome," so we sat down in front of a Zoom call and he goes, "I've handed in my notice to the board – effective immediately." We were all a bit shell-shocked. And then after a pause he added, "Oh and by the way, we've got the World Cup."'

Lloyd had started his job full of hope a couple of years before. He had been given a role in developing the game in his adopted home; a fresh start for him and for US cricket, it seemed. 'I think I was a little bit naive. I'm an optimist. I think the best of people and I'm a bit of an idealist. I honestly thought, "Iain Higgins – big name, coming from the ICC." We also had Richard Done, who was also joining as operations director and was a long-time servant from the ICC. We had Julie [Abbott] who was there on a part-time basis. We had Julia Price who was the women's head coach. We had the makings of a world class staff. I thought, "Wow, this is going to be something special." And because I'd done years of grind to the point of actually having a full-time job in cricket I was like, "Finally! The golden age is about to begin."

'I still knew we had a board who weren't great. But I guess I didn't think that they would be able to have the influence that they ended up having on the day-to-day operations.'

Lloyd's contention is that over time the USA Cricket board began to interfere more and more in affairs that were beyond their remit. He is one of several figures who found they were effectively being sidelined and ignored. 'Those of us who were staff were hired presumably because we were seen as experts in the field. But we were constantly not able to make decisions. We would have to present our ideas and

282

thoughts and they would get dissected and pulled apart and in the end the board would make the decisions.'

He gives one example of the formats for coaching junior cricket. 'I'm of the belief that smaller boundary sizes, smaller balls, smaller-length pitches are all a really important part of developing young players. Even when you introduce a hard ball should be later than we do. And the board pretty much feel the opposite – they want to get kids into hard-ball, full-size cricket as soon as possible because that's what Sachin Tendulkar did when he was a kid. I was constantly having that battle over this philosophy – which isn't mine by the way: it's something that's been proven across junior sport over a long period of time.

"Then there was the appointment of people across the country to local roles. If we did a regional women's tournament, we would appoint coaches and managers to those teams and Julie and myself were often involved in trying to promote certain individuals who had the right philosophy and the right skills. But it always felt like the board would sweep in and just put their own people into those positions, which really does impinge when I'm trying to build pathways, be it coaching education pathways, coaching pathways or player pathways.

'I'd run level one courses and we would talk about the philosophy and a player-centred approach and all this kind of stuff and you would encourage coaches to be that way and then those sort of coaches just wouldn't get the opportunities. In the end, at some of those courses, we were almost apologising to the coaches we were training saying, "Look, we believe that this is the right way to coach but we can't guarantee that it will actually end up in you getting opportunities because the board that I represent have their own ideas and their own agendas." It got laughable, some of the stuff that was going on.'

Despite this, for both men's and women's national teams, things seemed to be moving in the right direction. In December 2021 the USA faced Ireland in a T20 and ODI series at Broward County. Though the three ODIs were cancelled due to Covid, the USA won the first T20 as Gajanand Singh's 65 was enough to give the hosts a convincing 26-run victory.

Meanwhile, the women's national team were also winning matches. They swept through the Americas qualifier for the T20 World Cup in October 2021, winning five out of six games, many of them convincingly – Argentina were bowled out for just 47. Then in May 2022, the US women's team were one of five associates to be given ODI status. In their first ODI series against Zimbabwe in October 2024 they were only narrowly beaten by three games to two.

But by that point, Julia Price had gone and the West Indies legend Shiv Chanderpaul had taken over as the national coach. Julie Abbott is cynical about why the highly rated Aussie didn't have her contract renewed. 'The board love big names and I think the board members basically just wanted Shiv Chanderpaul there. There is a particular board member there who doesn't like powerful females involved at the top and that was part of the issue with her.'

Though results have kept improving, Abbott credits Price with making the difference: 'He [Chanderpaul] has reaped the benefit of all the work that Julia Price had done – hands down. There wasn't any competition for places. People just walked into the team because they'd always been part of the team. That was the expectation. They weren't training, they weren't high performers. And she changed that to a high performing environment, with a holistic programme. And that was never there before.

'Shiv is arguably one of the most fantastic batters that there has been in the history of cricket. But does that make him a great coach? He had no coaching experience when he came in and no coaching experience of women and girls either. And there were some controversial things with him also. The women's national team went out to Dubai to play in a World Cup qualifier and he didn't even go. He went out to the CPL instead. In the end at that point in time

USA Cricket was in such disarray – nobody was getting paid. I didn't get paid for almost a year and I know that Chanderpaul still wanted to book himself first-class tickets.'

Indeed, aside from the allegations of board interference, USA Cricket has been struggling for money. Badly. Much of this dates back to the deal made with American Cricket Enterprises, which came to light in 2022.

The document which was unearthed by *Cricinfo* in May that year revealed one of the most ludicrously one-sided deals in sporting history. It states that ACE gets to keep a whopping 95% of all cricket-related commercial revenue, in other words all the TV money, sponsorship money and gate receipts. USA Cricket is guaranteed a minimum amount, which in 2022 was just $399,000. The deal would need to generate $8 million to lift that amount and it has been nowhere near there since it was signed.

Whether this was naivety on behalf of the individuals who negotiated this or whether – as some rumours suggest – one of the figures concerned was provided with a generous back-hander to accept such a laughably unfair deal is something we'll never know. One thing is for sure. The people who have lost out are the ordinary cricketers of the US.

When the ODI series against Ireland had to be cut short due to Covid, USA Cricket lost out on over $250,000 in sponsorship and TV revenue, putting them deeply into debt. Staff were laid off and corners cut. 'I was part of a team that put together an entry-level programme,' remembers Jamie Lloyd. 'We developed all the resources. But because the budget got tight they said, "Sorry, that's it." We spent tens of thousands of dollars, getting a consultant in from Australia and putting together the branding and making the equipment but never getting the right level of funding to launch it properly. So that was hugely frustrating.'

To add to this the players weren't getting paid. The US national team players had been given central contracts prior to Covid, which with the highest at over $90,000 were the biggest among the associate nations. These were slashed by half during the pandemic. In an email to the USA Cricket board that was leaked to *Cricinfo* in July 2022, cricket committee member Vince Adams alleged that national team players had been waiting for their match fees for over a month: 'The habitual non-payment of players has been a major sore point for the [cricket committee], and we directed that it must be of the highest priority to ensure that players get their monies on time and must not be treated in any way differently to USAC's staff in this regard.'

He continued: 'It's a burning shame that all of the guardrails we put in place to make USAC a model operation representative of the greatest country, are so brazenly being torn down by this board.'

At the governing body's AGM in October 2022 the situation was made plain when it was announced that they would have to cancel that year's men's senior and under-19 national championships. USA Cricket had debts of over $650,000. One section of the budget showed that the organisation had wound up with $800,000 in administrative costs – over four times what it had budgeted for. No explanation was given for this huge overspending.

For long-time observers of US cricket this felt all too familiar. A broke governing body. An interfering board. Allegations of corruption. Peter Della Penna had long become cynical about the ongoing farce that was cricket in the USA.

'Gladstone Dainty was never the issue. He was the most visible representation of quite larger issues at a more local/regional level. He didn't vote himself into power. How did Gladstone Dainty get into power in the first place? Because everybody underneath voting for him was just as corrupt. Because there are so many bad characters and bad actors underneath, around him and supporting him.

'When the ICC wiped him out that didn't materially change all the other systemic issues that were a part of American cricket all round the country. Who did Gladstone

Dainty rise up against in the first place? He was a reaction to Atul Rai when he was president prior to Dainty – people talked about Atul Rai being a dictator and running American cricket like his own fiefdom. He installed all his cronies from Southern California who were part of his Indian club and Gladstone Dainty in 2003 was painted as "the saviour".

'Well in 2017 the ICC comes in as the white knight and removes Dainty. Well, who ran for the new board for USA Cricket? Atul Rai!

'He comes straight back with his cronies and Atul Rai not only runs but wins a seat on the board and the cycle repeats itself. After a short while Paraag Marathe is pushed out and who becomes chairman immediately after Paraag – Atul Rai becomes USA Cricket board chairman! In a sense he was a stop-gap, because the people who pushed Paraag out were Venu Pisike and Srini Salver. Essentially it was Venu out of Atlanta who was in a heated battle internally with Paraag. After Atul's usefulness runs out, Venu pushed him aside and Venu became the board chairman, essentially. And he has a couple of very loyal lieutenants who are running things.'

While all this politicking was going on, preparations were being made for the first Major League Cricket season. By March 2023 it had been confirmed that there would be six franchises initially, four of which would be owned by teams from the IPL. Kolkata Knight Riders took charge of the Los Angeles team, Chennai Super Kings snaffled up the Texas franchise, Delhi Capitals took on the Seattle Orcas and Mumbai Indians added New York to their portfolio of global franchises and named their team MI New York.

They had secured venues too, though from a projected eight venues around the country, this had been reduced to just two – Church Street Park in Morrisville, North Carolina and a new site in the suburbs of Dallas. Grand Prairie was a baseball venue known as Airhogs Stadium but had been bought by ACE in 2020 and renovated, with its capacity increased to 7,000. Interestingly, Broward County, the only ICC-certified ODI venue in the whole of the country, did not make the cut.

And there were a smattering of names from the wider world of cricket. In the player draft in March 2023 former South African captain Quinton de Kock joined Seattle Orcas, Australian opener Aaron Finch and ex-England man Liam Plunkett signed up for San Francisco Unicorns and Sri Lankan all-rounder Wanindu Hasaranga was drafted by Washington Freedom. Meanwhile, Jason Roy later had his central ECB contract torn up so he could play for Los Angeles Knight Riders.

Sunday, 30 July 2023, Grand Prairie Stadium, Texas. MLC final – MI New York v Seattle Orcas

So here it is, the climax to the tournament US cricket has been waiting for for years, for decades even. As I walk into the stadium I get accosted by a middle-aged white guy who thrusts a green Seattle Orcas flag into my hand. Then a woman doing exactly the same for MI New York sees me: 'Ah I can't say no now, can I?' I smile and accept her flag.

It's a shame that the local team – Texas Super Kings – were eliminated in the play-offs on Friday. But speaking to the MLC PR person earlier they were confident that this wouldn't affect ticket sales – most of the games at Grand Prairie have sold out, she says.

This evening is as hot as you'd expect Texas in late July to be. My laptop says it's 103 degrees outside at 7pm. Downstairs the crowd is gathering. There are families, gaggles of blokes in replica shirts, kids. Nearly all are of Asian extraction though there are a smattering of white faces here and there. There are stands of merch, people clutching 4 and 6 cards. Queues of kids patiently waiting to have their face painted.

Fifteen minutes before the start seven parachutists dive down on to the field, each one carrying a flag – six represent the MLC franchises with the final skydiver descending clutching the Stars and Stripes. All of them, thankfully, miss the wicket.

New York win the toss and put Seattle in to bat, with the first ball – apparently – being bowled by the Orcas' co-owner and Microsoft CEO Satya Nadella. The US anthem is sung by a girl soprano and everyone stands up (which was not the case during the play-off games) and there are the first of what will be several displays of fireworks tonight.

Quinton de Kock is the standout for the Orcas, hitting four sixes and nine boundaries in 52 balls before being clean bowled by New Zealander Trent Boult for 87. The very next ball Boult claims another, then two balls later one more. Seattle finish on 183.

During the interval there is a light show which is nothing less than amazing. Controlled by drones with lights attached, they initially lurk at the back of the stadium before coalescing to form the MLC logo, and then the logos of all the teams, a bowler, a batter and finally the words 'Cricket in the USA'. The crowd are as enchanted as British kids on bonfire night, as am I. It's a lovely touch that makes this even more of an event.

New York start their innings. After a slow first two overs the West Indian Nicholas Pooran gets his eye in and takes control. He hits a half-century off 16 balls – the quickest of the tournament. At the end of the powerplay MI are on 80/2 and way ahead of the required run rate.

In truth it's not much of a contest. Pooran hits an unbeaten 137 as New York ease home by six wickets and with four overs to spare. There are more fireworks. No less a luminary than Sunil Gavaskar is on hand to present the trophy to the winning team and among the MLC staff flitting to and fro around the venue there is a palpable sense of relief – mission complete.

And the people at the top seem happy. 'The US has emphatically shown the rest of the cricket world that it is capable of successfully hosting cricket of the highest calibre,' MLC co-founder Vijay Srinivasan says in an interview with the BBC after the game. It's true. It's finally happened.

* * *

Those in the stadium that night seemed happy – the vast majority of them were Texan cricket fans who had no stake in either team but who were there either to witness an historic sporting occasion or were simply delighted that they were able to see a decent game in the flesh. But there remain those who are sceptical about the true value of the MLC and question how much it is actually aiding the development of the game in the US, even if it is at all.

It's not just the unfair 95-5% profit share. There are questions about whether American players are being given the chance to show their talent. Unlike the ICC rules whereby a player has to be resident in a country for three years before they can represent their national team, the MLC have come up with their own definition of what constitutes a 'domestic player'. In the league's eyes it is anyone resident in the United States or anyone 'committed' to living in the US.

And so you have the ludicrous situation in which Liam Plunkett, who was part of England's 2019 World Cup winning team, is now a US domestic player. 'In season one you had situations where guys literally moved to the US three days before the draft having flaked out in India or Pakistan,' says Peter Della Penna. 'And MLC say, "Okay, you're eligible to be a domestic player now, you've shown you're committed in the space of 24 hours." It infuriated a lot of people.'

The counter-argument to that is that the cream always rises to the top and by fighting for their places 'real' US players are firing their irresolute clay. Nate Hays, the North Carolina-based writer and commentator, has gone back and forth on this issue. 'For a while I thought, like a lot of people, that the contracted players coming over for Major League Cricket would take away our cricketers' chances. I was in that camp. What made me change my mind was talking to the youngsters who started playing with these guys. They wanted to play with players of this calibre! They wanted to learn from Corey Anderson! They wanted to play with Liam Plunkett!

'So I saw how this was a good point. Sixteen first-class cricketers come and move to the USA to boost Major League Cricket – this is going to raise the standard of everybody, isn't it? And it has, plus it brings more attention to the project in general, which is a good thing.'

It remains to be seen whether the MLC investors are in for the long haul. To truly engage cricket fans all over the country, the event has to find new venues and expand beyond Texas. But in the second season, attendances were down on 2023. Whether that was merely a case of World Cup fatigue or a long-term problem is a question that will be answered in 2025. But the stadiums that were promised five years ago have yet to materialise, and it's doubtful potential investors in new venues will be impressed by the swathes of empty seats that were seen at Grand Prairie during MLC year two.

* * *

Meanwhile, USA Cricket was increasingly resembling the governing body of old. Jamie Lloyd paints a picture of a dysfunctional set-up run by a few key individuals who increasingly wanted to micro-manage all aspects of cricket in the country. 'It had been really traumatic for quite some time,' he said. 'The board had officially asked the CEO to fire me, just for trying to do my job the right way. I questioned whether we should be running certain events because we had no money and we owed people thousands of dollars and shouldn't we pay the people that we owe money to first? And I was told that I was "not supporting the board and its decisions" and all of that kind of stuff. It was just madness. I'm trying to be fiscally responsible, and I'm being told that I'm being a troublemaker.

'I'd seen my colleagues one by one get sawn off. Iain was the first to leave, of his own accord. Julia Price basically got told she wasn't wanted. They restructured things so she couldn't possibly stay onboard and that came from one board member in particular who wants to control the women's game. Richard Done got let go. Andrew Leonard got let go.'

Lloyd quit in early 2024 when he realised he wasn't even enjoying the cricket. 'We had a men's T20 nationals' tournament and myself and a couple of colleagues ran that whole tournament for five or six days and I realised about halfway through I just was not enjoying it at all. I was like, "Okay, this is a pretty good sign that I'm done."'

Meanwhile, as mandated by the ICC, USA Cricket had appointed a new CEO and it appeared that they had chosen well. As head of Afghanistan's cricket development department, Dr Noor Murad had been one of the key individuals behind that country's rapid rise to prominence in world cricket and full ICC membership. He was appointed as CEO in July 2023 but lasted just nine months.

Like everyone who enters the world of US cricket, Murad was full of plans and hope when he started the job. 'My vision for USA Cricket was rooted in strategic growth, professional governance, and global integration,' he tells us in an emailed interview. 'Upon assuming the role, I recognised the urgent need for a structured, transparent and forward-looking administration. Within my first three months, I led the development of a comprehensive five-year strategic plan [2024–2028], ensuring a sustainable roadmap for the growth of cricket in the US.'

However, Murad says that there was something ominous about what incoming USAC chairman Venu Pisike told him on his first day in the job. 'He said, "You were selected purely on merit, but the board and the community had expectations for someone from a specific country or region. I convinced the board, but I won't be able to convince the community. That's for you to handle." At first, I believed his words, as I had encountered similar dynamics in Afghanistan. However, over time, I realised the issue was not about the broader community but rather personal interests, favouritism, and other underlying motives. Leadership should be about vision, integrity, and serving the greater good and not catering to personal circles. My commitment has always been to transparency, inclusion, and the progress of the organisation as a whole.'

As Jamie Lloyd had already found out, USAC didn't want people who would act independently. They wanted yes men. 'I was expected to cater to political interests rather than lead independently. Over time, it became evident that a majority of the board, led by the chairman, prioritised political manoeuvring over cricket development, making governance extremely difficult.'

The points of disagreement soon became clear: '[There was] resistance to reforming the selection committee and establishing merit-based criteria. My efforts to implement structured financial and procurement policies were opposed by board members who preferred discretionary control. There was political interference – board members treated USA Cricket as a community club rather than a national governing body, prioritising personal interests over cricket's growth and my independence in securing sponsorships and negotiating international series agreements was met with hostility because it reduced board control over financial transactions.

'From the beginning, it became clear that certain board members believed they should control the day-to-day operations of USA Cricket, not for the betterment of the sport but to secure their personal interests. When I upheld financial transparency, governance principles and merit-based decision-making in selection, hiring, and finances, I was met with increasing hostility. The chairman and a few board members persistently pressured me to make politically motivated decisions, but I refused to compromise on meritocracy. This led to a complete breakdown in trust and a campaign to undermine my authority.'

Things came to a head, Murad alleges, when the USAC board started blocking the CEO's proposals, delaying funding and spreading misinformation about him. 'It was evident that my commitment to good governance had made me a target. At one point, I received a direct call from a board member just before an executive session, demanding that I terminate the contract of a long-serving staff member who had spoken out against their unconstitutional actions in the coaching selection process. In exchange, they implied that my own contract would be spared. I refused outright, questioning how they could expect me to betray my principles. Unbeknownst to me, they had already planned to call a board meeting to terminate my contract without cause.'

His contract was terminated, without an explanation. 'I only found out after the board meeting when I received a call from the chairman himself. While he acknowledged my technical expertise and management achievements, he admitted that I had failed to please certain board members, including himself. Shortly after, I received an email stating that my contract had been terminated without cause. I was then indirectly approached and told that if I agreed to obey whatever a few board members dictated, there was still time to reverse their decision. Until that moment, I had not even considered that my contract could be terminated, as I saw no valid reason. However, it turned out that they had structured a contract that allowed them to remove me without cause despite significant achievements in just a few months.'

Murad seems deeply shaken by the experience, describing the working environment as 'not only unprofessional but deeply toxic … I was subjected to immense mental stress and witnessed alarming behaviour that was eye-opening even for a system as structured as the USA's. Some board members openly admitted that I was being targeted because I was the only one who dared to challenge their unchecked control.

'I cannot disclose all the mistreatment I faced because no one would believe – especially in a country known for wisdom and freedom like the USA – how some individuals could act with such impunity. But this alone should tell you the story of how mismanaged USA Cricket was, where accountability was non-existent, and certain individuals felt emboldened to engage in discrimination and unethical practices simply to protect their personal gains.'

To lose one CEO was unfortunate, two careless, but lose three in the last 14 years and it looks as if American cricket has a systemic governance problem. Needless to say, we tried to contact USA Cricket in order to hear their side of this story. At the time of writing our email has yet to receive a response.

A long-time observer of American cricket like Della Penna simply rolls his eyes at the same pattern being repeated over and over and over again. 'It's just a pendulum swing, going the opposite way from what it was like 15 years ago. It was with Dainty and his West Indian bloc and everybody said "the problem is Dainty. Once you get rid of Dainty it'll be fine." Well, all it's resulted in is the pendulum swinging to a bunch of Indian administrators now and you've got a firm Indian bloc on the board, and they push all the buttons and control all the strings.'

He alleges that this extends into selection for the men's national team. 'So in the Dainty era, Steve Massiah was the one who was the puppet master. He was the captain. Everything ran through Steve Massiah. Dainty was the don and Massiah was one of his capos. But Massiah had a huge amount of influence in terms of who got in the team. If Massiah didn't like you, you didn't have a shot at getting into the national team. And, more often than not, when push came to shove and there was a 50-50 selection call it would come down to who Massiah liked. And generally speaking, he would side with a West Indian heritage player.

'And now the pendulum is swinging the other way. The Indians are in control of the board. You've got an Indian captain and when push comes to shove at selection and you've got a choice between player A and B, the selection battle will go to the player of Indian heritage.'

He cites two examples of this: Ravi Timbawala and Srini Salver. Back in 2009 Timbawala, he argues, was the best young batsman in America. 'He was 20 or 21 at the time. I thought he was the standout player of that era. He probably should have been picked to play for the USA at that time. Who got picked instead? Steven Taylor. Steven Taylor was 16 years old, five years younger than Timbawala. Very promising talent, no doubt. But he's 16 and still very raw. Why did Taylor get the nod? You could argue because he has West Indian heritage.

'Ravi Timbawala did eventually get to play for the USA but was way past his prime, after he had sustained a significant injury. In the summer of 2014 he tore an ACL.

He came back and got picked to play for the USA in 2016 but by that stage I felt he was well past his peak. He gets picked right when the regime change starts to happen. Steven Taylor was captain at the time. Massiah is out of the picture. USACA was suspended. ICC is in charge of things. Timbawala only lasts in the team for one or two tournaments and then he gets dropped.

'And now Ravi Timbawala is the selection chair. So now it's payback time, if I read between the lines of what's going on currently. Ravi Timbawala and Srini Salver, who is on the board, are former players. There's two simultaneous threads here. First Timbawala – he didn't get picked when he should have. He's now taken a vantage point, as far as I can see, as "all the times that Indian guys shouldn't have been picked and got snubbed, well now that I'm in charge I'm going to make sure that Indian guys get picked". Screw everybody else. And that's exactly what's happening.'

Meanwhile Salver, Della Penna alleges, is working through resentment at his own mistreatment when he was in the national team. When he broke through in 2018, the official national team policy was that players – no matter their standing, skill or where in the world they were based – would have to show their 'commitment' to Team USA by attending national trials. 'It didn't matter if you were a passport holder or living overseas – nobody was getting special treatment.

'So what happened? Srini Salver goes to the regional trials, gets picked for the national trial, does well enough there and gets picked for the USA to play in the T20 Americas qualifier in North Carolina. Subsequently they were going to go to the Super 15 in Barbados and then from there they were going to go to WCL in Oman and that was going to be the key to get ODI status.'

But breaking this new rule, Aaron Jones, a batsman who was born in New York, and leg-spinner Hayden Walsh Junior, both of whom had already represented Barbados, were called into the US squad for the games in Oman after impressing in the nets. Srini was one of many fringe players who were not impressed.

'Srini says, "For the last nine months you were chewing my ear off about 'commitment commitment, nobody gets special treatment'. This guy Aaron Jones shows up to one nets session and you fast track him into the USA squad, taking my spot. What the hell?" And the coach Pubudu [Dassanayake] shrugs his shoulders and says, "Well we need to win. We have to get ODI status. ODI status is going to fund everything else going forward. If you want to get ODI status, I have to make this exception. Sorry." So Salver gets dropped for doing this.'

However, in 2020 Srini runs for the position of player representative on the USAC board. 'Ever since then he's been hellbent on getting retribution for how he was treated,' says Della Penna. 'He has come in [onto the USAC board] and guys who are US passport holders like Brody Couch, who's doing incredibly now in first-class cricket for Western Australia and has a dual US/Australia passport. And there are Cameron Gannon and Cameron Stevenson – guys who are US-eligible who are passport holders who are playing arguably a much higher standard of cricket overseas than in the US. The coach Stuart Law wanted to pick Brody Couch and Cameron Stevenson for the T20 World Cup but Srini Salver said, "No. We're not playing these guys unless they show up to a trial in Texas. They have to show their commitment."

'All this is because of what Srini went through. "This is how I got dropped. I'm not going to let it happen to anybody else. I'm standing up for the local guys." Local, by Srini's manipulated definition, is anybody of Indian heritage. But if you're of a different heritage, domestically in the US, you're not getting picked. And if you're overseas you're definitely not getting picked.'

All of which made for an unpromising backdrop to the T20 World Cup in June 2024, the first such event to be (partly, at least) held on American soil.

Saturday, 1 June 2024: United States v Canada, T20 World Cup

When I arrived yesterday at Dallas I told the immigration officer I was here to watch the cricket. The comment barely registered with him. I'd be surprised if he even knew what cricket is, let alone that there is a World Cup in the sport happening right now. It's the day after President Trump has been found guilty in the hush money case and America clearly has its mind on other things.

In the press there have been rumours that the 7,000-capacity stadium hasn't been sold out and the weather has been hit and miss. This afternoon brought a heavy downpour to Grand Prairie and on TV there were thunderstorm warnings for much of the Dallas area while I watched the Champions League final in my hotel room.

By the time early evening arrives, the weather has cleared and there are blue skies. As I arrive at the stadium Beyonce's *Texas Hold 'Em* is playing, appropriately. I look around at the crowd – the demographics are much the same as the Major League final last year: around 85% South Asian extraction with a smattering of white and other minorities here and there. A few have turned up in US shirts, but probably more have either India or Pakistan, or one of the IPL franchises. The toss is overseen by (match referee) Richie Richardson. The USA win and elect to put Canada in to bat first.

Before play starts there are fireworks and then a marching band in pink and blue livery appear. Unusually for a band they don't appear to be playing their instruments – the music appears to be coming through the PA system. Some of the band do somersaults and then some of them split off and wave pink streamers about. It's then it occurs to me that this must be what passes for an opening ceremony.

The tournament mascots come our way and they resemble smurfs wearing shades, except one is red as well as blue. They wave at the crowd, who seem quietly bemused by all this. It's hardly IPL levels of razzmatazz. A quartet of people with what seem like fire extinguishers on their backs a la *Ghostbusters* appear on the other side of the ground. They let out streams of dry ice from their canisters. There are more fireworks. On the other side members of the marching band appear to be attempting to breakdance.

Finally the kids with the flags come on to the pitch to remind us that there is an international cricket match going on today – indeed the oldest international fixture in the world. People around me stand up for the anthems and yes you can't help but get a lump in your throat during the *Star Spangled Banner*. Even despite everything – the dubious 'patriotism' of the MAGA movement, the division and deterioration of public debate – America as an idea, that appeals to mankind's greater purpose, retains its power. Looking around at the South Asian Americans saluting their anthem, holding up their flags and in some cases singing, you can't help but feel moved.

But that said, there are plenty of unsold seats. The ground is only around two-thirds full and clearly USA v Canada has not captured the locals' imagination as the Major League final did last year.

Finally, there is cricket. Canada get off to a flying start. Their first ball goes for four and they quickly build some momentum.

'Can we get some chanting going, guys?' asks a fellow in the front row. And indeed there is some desultory 'U-S-A!' chanting. Followed by another boundary. And another. 'Maybe if we chant "Canada they'll get a wicket," suggests one wag. After four overs they already have 40.

USA struggle to get a handle on the Canadian batters. Steven Taylor is expensive as a bowler. Two of his first three balls go for six and after ten overs Canada are 85/2.

Every so often the cameras head to the perimeter and, as they come into view, the crowd oblige with 'U-S-A' chants. Another observation – the US fielding is probably the best that I have ever seen. It's so much sharper and quicker than at any time in the last 20 years. They're accurate and economical in their throwing in a way they certainly were not in the old days.

Canada finish on 194/5. A tall order, over nine an over.

The USA's innings couldn't have got off to a worse start. Having waited for so long to make his debut in a major tournament Steven Taylor is out first ball lbw even before much of the crowd have returned to their seats. The US take until the sixth ball to finally get off the mark.

In front of me a young lad is chanting 'U-S-A'. He's dressed in an India shirt. Dual identities in action. But the crowd can sense that this match is already slipping away from the US – the required run rate is around 12 per over. One guy gets a chant going: 'We want sixes! We want sixes!' And almost inevitably the US lose a wicket.

But then something stirs. Aaron Jones, who's been out there since the first over having replaced Taylor, starts to make his presence felt. In the ninth over the crowd finally see their first six, courtesy of Andries Gous. Then he and Jones start going about their business. He cracks 50 off just 22 balls – the fastest half-century in US history.

The 14th over is the turning point. Gous is caught and is already walking towards the pavilion when it is revealed that it was a no-ball. Off the next delivery Jones serenely knocks another six – his eighth. By now those 'U-S-A' chants are being sung with conviction, with gusto.

Gous finally goes on 65 and Corey Anderson, the New Zealander who has switched sides to represent his new country, arrives to guide USA over the line. Inevitably, it's Jones who delivers the knockout punch in the 18th over, with his tenth six. He's scored 94 not out off a mere 40 balls. He sinks to the ground, stretching his arms to the sky in victory. He's made history.

It's not just the greatest moment in US T20 history – it's one of the greatest in all T20 history. Only Chris Gayle has hit more sixes in one innings at the T20 World Cup. His third-wicket partnership with Gous was worth 131 runs off just 58 balls.

But the families who exit the stadium beaming with delight aren't thinking about cold stats. As I leave I can hear one teenage girl say to another, 'I want Jones's autograph. He said hi to me when he was on the boundary!' I pop into the merch shop on the way out and I can see people picking up USA shirts.

Afterwards Jones downplays his achievement, although he can't help slipping in that: 'Hopefully tonight's innings will probably open the eyes of those who don't know me or USA cricket. We have great players here and we have a lot of talent here.'

Tonight, perhaps for the first time since the days of John Bart King, the United States finally has a cricketing hero.

Thursday, 6 June 2024: United States v Pakistan, T20 World Cup

As the mean old Texas sun beats down, there's undeniable excitement as I enter Grand Prairie stadium. But it's a complicated excitement. The victory over Canada doesn't seem to have overnight produced a fresh generation of fans cheering on the USA. It's green Pakistan shirts that outnumber USA blue shirts by ten to one.

The US fans from Saturday have evaporated. But of course they could be the same people – it's just that loyalties to the old country have trumped their adopted home. There are plenty of folks flaunting their dual identities here. One woman's T shirt reads 'I may live in the USA but my story began in Pakistan'. Many others here today will nod in recognition at those words.

That said, the only US player who gets even a flutter of a cheer is Aaron Jones. In contrast the cheers for the Pakistan line-up are loud and hearty.

The US get off to a flying start. In the second over left-arm seamer Netravalkar steams in, there's a snick and Steven Taylor takes a spectacular catch. The stadium DJ plays the Backstreet Boys' *Bye Bye Bye*. A few souls start a 'U-S-A! U-S-A!' chant.

Incredibly in the next over they grab another. Usman Khan's lofted shot is caught comfortably on the boundary by

Kumar. This isn't going to the script – 14/2. Pakistan can't get a grip – their run rate is below six. There's another lofted shot and another easy catch for Taylor. 'We're about to lose to the USA.' Already Pakistan fans are having an inquest. It's 26/3. The grumbles of frustration grow louder. The run rate is below five. 'This is embarrassing,' one Pakistan fan says. But in this heat, the US bowling attack begins to tire and eventually boundaries and sixes start to arrive. The crowd go predictably crazy as Pakistan start to find the gaps. A budding entrepreneur mingles amongst the crowd: 'Cold beer, cold beer' he calls out, only to get short shrift from the Pakistan fans. 'Haram, haram.'

Then just as they start to get going there's another wicket. Shadab Khan is caught on 40. It's 98/4. Next ball Azam Khan is out lbw. Then in the 15th over another lbw. 'Come on 160, 160!' is the cry behind me, a sign of the diminished expectations.

In the end they can't even reach that. Pakistan finish on 159. They've looked arrogant, as if all they had to do to win was turn up. But the USA aren't the pushovers they used to be. They bowled and fielded tightly and Pakistan now know they're in a game.

The USA get off to a decent start. Steven Taylor cracks a third-ball boundary. Mohammad Amir's first two balls are wides. Third over and USA are already on

24. Pakistan review for an lbw but even from here it didn't look out.

Pakistan get a breakthrough in the sixth over. Steven Taylor goes for 12 as he edges to Muhammad Rizwan. Their fans go crazy around me. 'Now we can begin to show our quality,' one says.

They almost get Gous next ball, but his shot just eludes Ifkithar at slip. Pakistan's 'quality' isn't showing yet. Too many balls are full tosses or are too short. Gous scores a couple more boundaries and a six. There are mutterings of discontent once more among the Pakistan fans.

After ten overs USA are 76/1. Monack Patel gets his eye in too – and reaches his fifty off just 34 balls. And there's still Jones to come. Pakistan need a couple of wickets fast.

They get a breakthrough at the start of the 14th as Gous is clean bowled by Haris Rauf. USA need just 56 off 41 balls. Next over Patel goes for 50. This is going to be tight. In the 16th over Jones displays the sort of hitting that made him a hero on Saturday with a six lofted into the crowd. The USA now need 35 from 26 balls.

It gradually dawns on the crowd that we're witnessing an incredible game, an historic game. There are noises of due appreciation for the USA team, as much as ones disparaging Pakistan. And what if it's a tie? For the first time today the phrase 'super over' can be heard among the crowd. As the number of balls left dwindles one by one, time too slows down. 20 from 11 balls. 19 from 10. 19 from 9. 18 from 8.

With one over left USA need 15. Some brilliant running from Jones and Nitish Kumar ekes out three runs. With three balls left USA need 12. Jones slams a six, then gets a single. And then Kumar hits a boundary with the last ball. A super over. Everyone is going crazy around me.

USA go first. Interestingly Harmeet Singh has been chosen to bat, alongside Jones. Mohammad Amir is bowling. Jones hits a boundary first ball, then two and then a single. But Amir gives away two wides. There are groans of disappointment. Then another. And in the midst of this they give away another run when there's an overthrow. USA score 18.

Netravalkar is bowling for the USA. Pakistan score a boundary second ball. But then Iftikar is caught and after an agonisingly long review it's confirmed: out. Surely USA can't let this slip from here?

Not this time. Netravalkar concedes a boundary. But no more. They've done it. USA have beaten Pakistan. A good percentage of Pakistan's fans file out, many gesticulating, not quite believing what they've seen. A number of them stay and applaud the USA team who are carrying Netravalkar on their shoulders. This is the moment American cricket has waited so, so long for. There's still India and Ireland to play. But even if they lose those, by winning today and against Canada they have achieved a level of respectability at the T20 World Cup and shown the whole world they really can play cricket.

* * *

This, then, is the happy ending we had always wanted for our odyssey … wasn't it? Except unlike Homer's work this isn't fiction. Real life doesn't tend to have neat resolutions.

The events of that day in Texas had a heat haze unreality to them, but even as the fans, the press and ICC staff were fanning out of Grand Prairie, US cricket was still showing its unerring ability to snatch misfortune from the jaws of triumph.

Monank Patel, the captain whose fifty had been so vital to the victory, started drinking and injured himself. 'The version of the story that I've heard is that in a drunken state he was climbing on top of one of the seats on the team bus, fell over and landed on his shoulder,' says Della Penna. 'He went to hospital and it showed it was a hairline shoulder fracture. It was abundantly clear it was not going to be healed in time for the rest of the tournament.'

The obvious thing would be to call up another player. That, however, did not happen. 'Stuart Law [the coach] wanted to replace him. But the board members that he

[Patel] is cosy with said, "No, no, no. You're not replacing him, he's our captain." So what did Monank do? He travelled with the rest of the team for the rest of the tournament and had a free vacation.'

In their next match, up in New York at the pop-up stadium which the ICC, in their wisdom, had decided to build specifically for the tournament, the US were (as expected) soundly beaten by India. It all came down to the last game against Ireland at Broward County. Somehow the USA's luck was in that day as rain ensured no play, which meant one point for both sides. Somehow the US were through to the second stage of the competition: the Super 8s.

After that the team's World Cup campaign petered out somewhat. They were competitive against South Africa in the first game, only losing by 18 runs. But both West Indies and England beat them with some ease. No matter. To be there was enough – it ensures that the United States have already qualified for the next T20 World Cup in India and Sri Lanka in 2026.

But chaos and dysfunction still stalks US cricket. Just weeks after the World Cup, the ICC put USAC on notice, which is the first step before another suspension. One of the issues – the fact that there was, yet again, a vacancy in the CEO position – was put right when it was announced in July

2024 that the supremo of US Rugby, Johnathan Atkeison, had been appointed to the position. By October, Stuart Law, the coach who had steered the US to those victories against Canada and Pakistan, was dismissed. He had lasted just seven months in the post. No explanation was given, but rumours abound that his deteriorating relationship with the untouchable captain Monank Patel was a major factor.

When asked, every player, administrator, writer or broadcaster we've interviewed on this long journey, has said that they are 'hopeful' about the future of US cricket. Perhaps you have to be by definition, operating in a sporting subculture that takes its marginality for granted. Likewise, nobody from the ICC and the cricket moguls of the IPL right down to the bumbling cricket entrepreneurs and the ordinary players at grass roots level has ever disagreed about its huge potential. One day both hope and potential will be fulfilled. What keeps everyone going are those moments when the sunshine peeks through the clouds and you can see how good US cricket could be, when an Aaron Jones or an Andries Gous casually swats a Mohammad Amir delivery to the boundary like it's the most natural thing in the world.

'They have pushed cricket into people's minds,' said Nate Hays when we met him after the World Cup. 'They have advanced cricket in the US faster just by winning a couple of games than anything anybody else could have done, even if it was done well. Just because of that, they're heroes. Just by playing the game well, winning and being fearless and being brave. Just by doing something people didn't think they could do, just by doing that they have done what our board could never do. So that's why I'm optimistic. Because we are actually good.'

And now it's time for us to part. Our journey is over, but US cricket's odyssey continues on into the second quarter of the 21st century. Its future will depend on whether it manages to effectively harness the energy, enthusiasm and talent of those who reside among its grassroots and whether their passion and skill eventually hold sway over the self-serving venality of those who purport to run the game.

We know which side we're on.